DEVONPORT DOCKYARD RAILWAY

DEVONPORT DOCKYARD RAILWAY

BY
PAUL BURKHALTER

TWELVEHEADS PRESS

TRURO 1996

CONTENTS

INTRODUCTION		5
Chapter One	THE VICTORIAN DOCKYARD	7
Chapter Two	THE TUNNEL	9
Chapter Three	FIRST RAILWAYS IN THE DOCKYARD	15
Chapter Four	CONNECTION TO THE CORNWALL RAILWAY	21
Chapter Five	LATE NINETEENTH CENTURY EXTENSIONS TO THE DOCKYARD	45
Chapter Six	INTO THE TWENTIETH CENTURY	57
Chapter Seven	THE PASSENGER TRAIN SERVICE	71
Chapter Eight	FREIGHT	75
Chapter Nine	MAIN LINE SIGNALLING & BRANCH OPERATION	79
Chapter Ten	INTERNAL SIGNALLING & OPERATION	83
Chapter Eleven	MAIN LINE SERVICES	87
Chapter Twelve	PERMANENT WAY	93
Chapter Thirteen	THE LOCOMOTIVES	97
Chapter Fourteen	ROLLING STOCK	131
Chapter Fifteen	RAILGAUGE SHUNTING CRANES	139
Appendix One	TUNNEL BELL SIGNALS	142
Appendix Two	NAVY ESTIMATES 1854 to 1935	142
Appendix Three	TABLE OF FREIGHT SHIPMENTS	144
Appendix Four	LSWR 1919 INSTRUCTIONS	144
Appendix Five	TABLE OF LOCOMOTIVES	145
Appendix Six	TABLE OF ROLLING STOCK	147
Appendix Seven	TABLE OF SHUNTING CRANES	148
SOURCES & ACKNOWLEDGEMENTS		150
INDEX		151

FRONT COVER TOP: Passenger train at South Yard terminus. COLLECTION P. BURKHALTER

FRONT COVER (BOTTOM): No 18 in March 1963. B. MILLS

BACK COVER: No. 18 January 1963. P GRAY

FRONTICE:
The passenger train on 27 March 1963 at the stop outside Central Offices in North Yard. Behind the last carriage is the tunnel mouth, beneath the entrance gatehouse at the foot of Albert Road. L CROSIER

All rights reserved. No part of this publication may be reproduced or transmitted in any form or by any means without the prior permission of the publisher.

© Paul Burkhalter 1996.

TWELVEHEADS PRESS

First published 1996 by Twelveheads Press, Chy Mengleth, Twelveheads, Truro, Cornwall TR4 8SN.

ISBN 0 906294 37 1
British Library Cataloguing-in-Publication Data.
A cataogue record for this book is available from the British Library.

Designed by Alan Kittridge
Printed by The Amadeus Press Ltd., Huddersfield.

This book encompasses the railways that served what is now known as Devonport Royal Dockyard. Over the centuries other titles have been given for various parts of the establishment, and a short list follows. However for ease the general title of Devonport Dockyard has been used to describe the whole location, but individual names are used where appropriate.

Original Name	**Current Name**
Devonport Yard	South Yard
Gun Wharf	Morice Yard
Keyham Steam Yard	North Yard
Extension Yard	North Yard
RN Barracks Keyham	HMS Drake

INTRODUCTION
ORIGINS AND EARLY YEARS OF THE DOCKYARD

In Henry II's reign the small huddle of houses around Sutton Pool, to the east of Plymouth's present City Centre, was described as 'a mene thing as a inhabitation for Fischars'. A hundred years later in 1295, after the French King tried to seize English possessions in France, King Edward I assembled a fleet at Plymouth for an expedition in retaliation. This could be said to be the start of Plymouth's long association with the Navy. Charles II sailed up the 'Hamoss' (Hamoaze) to see for himself potential sites for a naval base in the company of Samuel Pepys, who was Secretary of the Navy, but this came to naught. However it was William II who directed that a site be found on the Western Approaches, and so began the story of Devonport Dockyard.

Many of the ports of Devon came under scrutiny, but the Admiralty finally decided upon Plymouth. The eastern arm of the Sound at Cattewater was first considered, then a site at Saltash, but that plan was abandoned too. Then after a survey of all the inlets from the Sound the Surveyor of the Navy, Edward Dummer, urged that the new dockyard be placed in the Hamoaze. (Hamoaze is the name of the lower reaches of the River Tamar above its outlet to Plymouth Sound.)

On 3 December 1690 a contract was signed with Robert Waters of Portsmouth to construct a stone dock at Point Froward (in the centre of the present day South Yard) to accommodate a third rate ship, for the sum of £11,000. What was significant about this was that the construction was to be of stone. Hitherto all Naval dry docks had been built in wood, with the obvious disadvantage of a short life span. Almost immediately Dummer

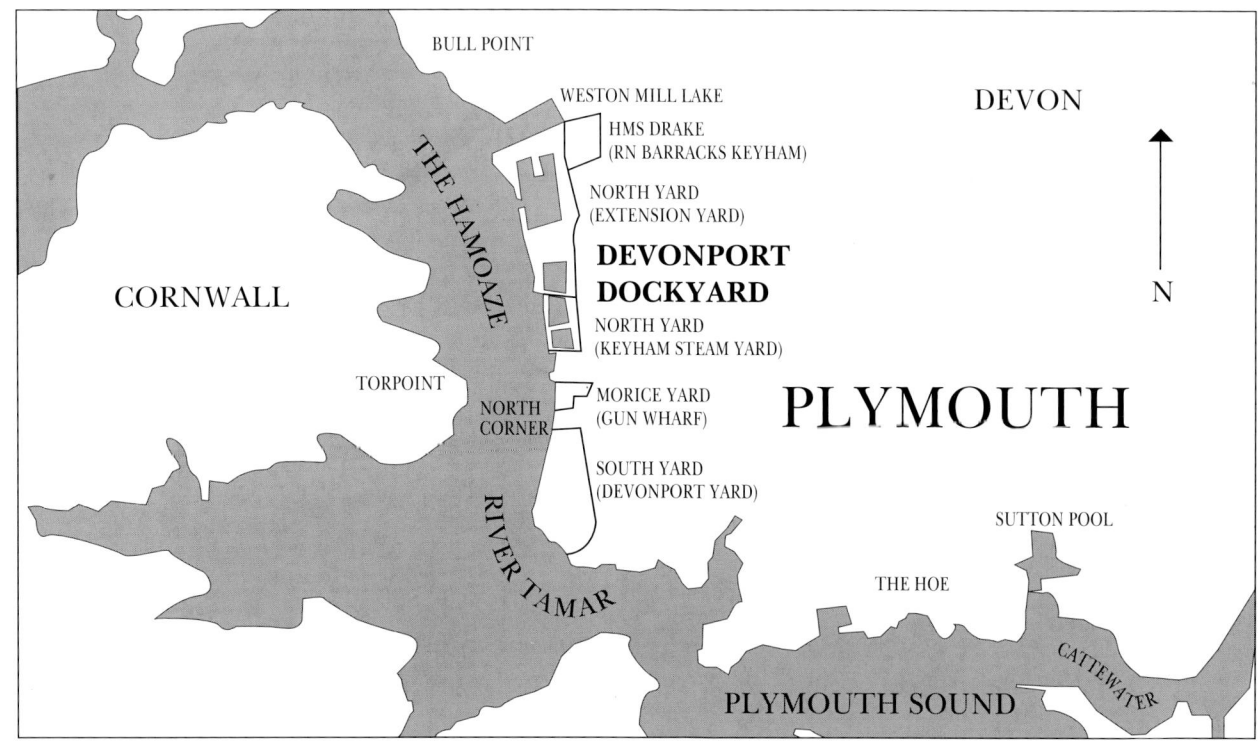

put forward a revised plan to extend the scheme by including a wet basin and a larger dry dock. This was approved by the King with the proviso that the dock accommodate a ship the size of a first rate. Waters was again contracted for the work, which by now was to cost £50,000 including residences, stores and workshops. The dock was finished by the end of 1692, with the other structures gradually following until 1697.

The first workers numbered 75 and were accommodated in hulks moored in the river. The nearest houses were in the town of Plymouth, some two miles distant within the old town walls. However by 1700 the first houses in the immediate area were appearing at North Corner (Cornwall Beach), and grew rapidly in number, until in 1731 the size of the community was approaching that of a small town. This turned out to be an unwise choice of location, as we shall see later, but led, indirectly, to the *raison d'etre* for the railway.

The residents of Plymouth, away over the hill, looked down on the 'Dockers', little realising that the industry growing there would have such an impact in the centuries to come.

To the north of the houses at North Corner the Ordnance Department acquired a 4 acre site in 1718 for the purposes of a weapons depot, known as 'Gun Wharf'. Constructed there were storehouses, workshops for gun carriages, a powder magazine and a cooperage. Between 1720 and 1723 a row of houses for the Officers, which still stand to this day, were erected on high ground to the rear of the site.

At about this time further expansion enlarged the Yard and, indeed, over the rest of the eighteenth century much work was done to improve and extend the facilities. Acts of Parliament in 1758 and 1766 paved the way for fortifications to be thrown up around the Yard in its defence, although it was 1853 before they were seriously completed. Bearing the name Plymouth Dock the locality grew in population until in 1837 it exceeded the size of Plymouth. In 1824 the name Devonport received Royal approval although it was not until 1841 that Plymouth Yard changed its name to Devonport Yard.

The community at Cornwall Beach – the 'North Corner' of the original dockyard, pictured c. 1910.
A KITTRIDGE COLLECTION

CHAPTER ONE

THE VICTORIAN DOCKYARD

The move from sail power to the new technology of the nineteenth century revolutionised the propulsion of ships on the high seas, although for many years ships were fitted out with both steam engines and rigging for sail. In the early part of the century only smaller tugs and the like were exclusively steam and it was not until September 1831 that the first steam fighting ship was laid down at Plymouth Yard. A paddle vessel named *Rhadamanthus*, she was floated out of dock on 16 April 1832, although the engines were actually fitted at Woolwich.

From these early days to the middle years of the nineteenth century there was a large increase in the number of steam driven ships of all sizes. Many were conversions from sail craft; ten large ships being so treated at Devonport between 1852 and 1860.

This rapid expansion of the steam fleet sorely taxed the capability of the old yards. Indeed the lack of capacity at Devonport forced the Navy to send ships to Portsmouth and to Woolwich for repairs. Expansion was necessary but Devonport Yard had now been entirely surrounded by civilian development and, with the growing size of vessels and with differing needs, something had to be done to provide new facilities.

The only place to go was northwards, up the Hamoaze. But immediately to the north housing reached down to the waters edge at Cornwall Beach. Beyond was the Gun Wharf depot of the Ordnance Department, and further north still were some powder magazines at Keyham Point.

After a detailed survey of both sides of the Hamoaze, a site was selected half a mile upstream from the north wall of the existing Yard. Thirty-eight acres of land, plus forty-three acres of foreshore, were bought from the Trustees of the will of Sir John St Aubyn to add to the land already occupied by the Keyham Point Powder store. This latter facility was moved further north to Bullpoint, beyond Weston Mill Lake, so clearing the way for a new modern yard, built specifically for the ships of the future.

Here it is proposed to construct two floating basins about six acres each, with entrances 80 feet wide, laid at a depth sufficient for the largest steamer to enter and depart at all times of the tide, there are to be three large docks. There are to be complete engine and boiler workshops with the requisite tools and storehouses for fitting out and repairing large fleets of steamers, the whole establishment will cover about 72 acres.

Sir John Rennie is credited with designing some of the facilities of the new estate created at the new location at Keyham.

The foundation stone was laid by the Rt. Hon. the Earl of Auckland, GCB, then First Lord of the Admiralty, on 12 September 1846. It comprised a nine ton block of granite in which had been placed a box containing the current coins of the realm. However work had actually been started two years earlier by Messrs Geo. Baker & Sons, who first made use of Nasmyth's steam hammer to install a lengthy caisson, or artificial wall, around the river side of the site, so as to exclude the water to provide a dry area in which to work. The original contract value as proposed by Baker was £713,000, already somewhat in excess of the first estimate of £400,000. By 1849 this had risen to £1,322,627, and it is no wonder that Parliament was less than pleased. Excavation from the area within the cofferdam was taken to the north of the site to be dumped in Keyham Creek (where St Levans Road is now), whilst that from outside the caisson was taken by barge to fill holes near Drake's Island, in Plymouth Sound.

A great retaining wall rose at the east of

the site, dug into the hill of Keyham, which allowed a level area for the workshops and offices. The principal building, however, was the Quadrangle, an area of about six acres, designed by Charles Barry, who at the time was heavily involved in the lengthy and troubled construction of the Houses of Parliament. The Quadrangle was the heart of the new complex, named Keyham Steam Yard, with all the facilities to support the new steam navy; boiler shops, plater's shop, millwrights and pattern shop, brass foundry, coppersmiths and blacksmiths, and the fitting and erecting area close by.

The docks and basins were flooded in May 1853 and the whole complex opened officially on 7 October 1853. So was completed the magnificent new arrangement for the upkeep of the modern Victorian Navy. It provided employment for almost 2,000 and hence became the largest employer in the south west of England.

1854 Act of Parliament for the tunnel.

ANNO DECIMO SEPTIMO

VICTORIÆ REGINÆ.

C A P. XV.

An Act to empower the Commissioners of the Admiralty to construct a Tunnel between Her Majesty's Dockyard at *Devonport* and Her Majesty's Steam Factory Yard at *Keyham*, and to acquire certain Property for Her Majesty's Service.   [2d *June* 1854.]

WHEREAS it is expedient that the Commissioners for executing the Office of Lord High Admiral of the United Kingdom of *Great Britain* and *Ireland* should be empowered to make and construct a Communication between Her Majesty's Dockyard at *Devonport* and Her Majesty's Steam Factory Yard at *Keyham*, by means of a Tunnel, or partly by a Tunnel and partly by open Cutting, for the exclusive Use of Her Majesty's Service, and that the said Commissioners should be empowered to acquire the Fee Simple of all such Portions of the said Dockyard at *Devonport*, and the Use in perpetuity of the Roadways, Ways, and Passages in connexion therewith the Fee Simple of which may not now be vested in Her Majesty, or in the said Commissioners in trust for Her Majesty, Her Heirs and Successors, for the Public Service, and also the Fee Simple of certain Lands at or near the Entrance of the said Steam Factory Yard at *Keyham*, mentioned or referred to in the

3 A   Second

CHAPTER TWO
THE TUNNEL

The new establishment of Keyham Steam Yard was detached from the existing facilities by a distance of half a mile. In the intervening area was the access road to the Torpoint Ferry, the floating bridge to Cornwall, the Gun Wharf (run by the Army), a heavily populated part of the town and quite a hill jutting out toward the river bank.

At the earliest stages of planning for the new Keyham Yard it was decided to include a tunnel between the two establishments. The entrance and gatehouses at the bottom of Albert Road was one of the early structures started in 1849 and had the first section of tunnel built into the foundations.

As the Admiralty tunnel was to pass under civil property an Act of Parliament was required. Deposited with the Clerk of the Peace for Devon on 25 November 1853 'at a quarter to ten in the forenoon', this was brought to the House of Commons on 7 February 1854 by Sir James Graham and Messrs Cowper and Osbourne, respectively

Tunnel Act plans

PROPOSED TUNNEL
FROM
Keyham Steam Yard to Her Majesty's Dock Yard
DEVONPORT

PLANS & SECTIONS
1853.4

W. DAMANT, PLYMOUTH.

WATERLOW & SONS, LITHOGRAPHERS & ENGRAVERS,
65 to 68, London Wall, & 49 Parliament Street, London.

the Secretary of the Admiralty (and MP for Middlesex), the Deputy Lieutenant for Kent and the Member for Carlisle. It proceeded through the Reading and Committee stages and was referred to the Upper House on 28 April. The Lords pondered over the lack of mention of expense of the works and that there was no reference to the funding of the project, but concluded that as it was a Government sponsored work this was not necessary. However their Lordships did consider the occupants of the property that would be affected by the tunnel works, for it was recorded that 121 houses containing 1,601 persons 'of the labouring classes' in the streets between Devonport and Keyham Yards fell into this category. Also listed were 44 shops, and five pubs or beerhouses. But the provisions of the Bill allowed compensation so without amendment it passed through and received their agreement on 18 May 1854.

Royal Assent for the Bill was granted on 2 June 1854, which empowered 'the Commissioners of the Admiralty to construct a Tunnel between Her Majesty's Dockyard at Devonport and Her Majesty's Steam Factory Yard at Keyham, and to acquire certain Property for Her Majesty's Service'.

In the text of the Act the alternatives of either an open cutting or a mixture of tunnel and cutting would have been permitted. Other provisions included the powers to:
Lay down and work a railway
Divert and reinstate a range of existing public works from gas pipes to sewers
Pay compensation
Maintain the footpaths in Moon Street.

Other conditions applied. Moon Cove, an inlet off the Hamoaze adjacent to the north

Tunnel Act plans

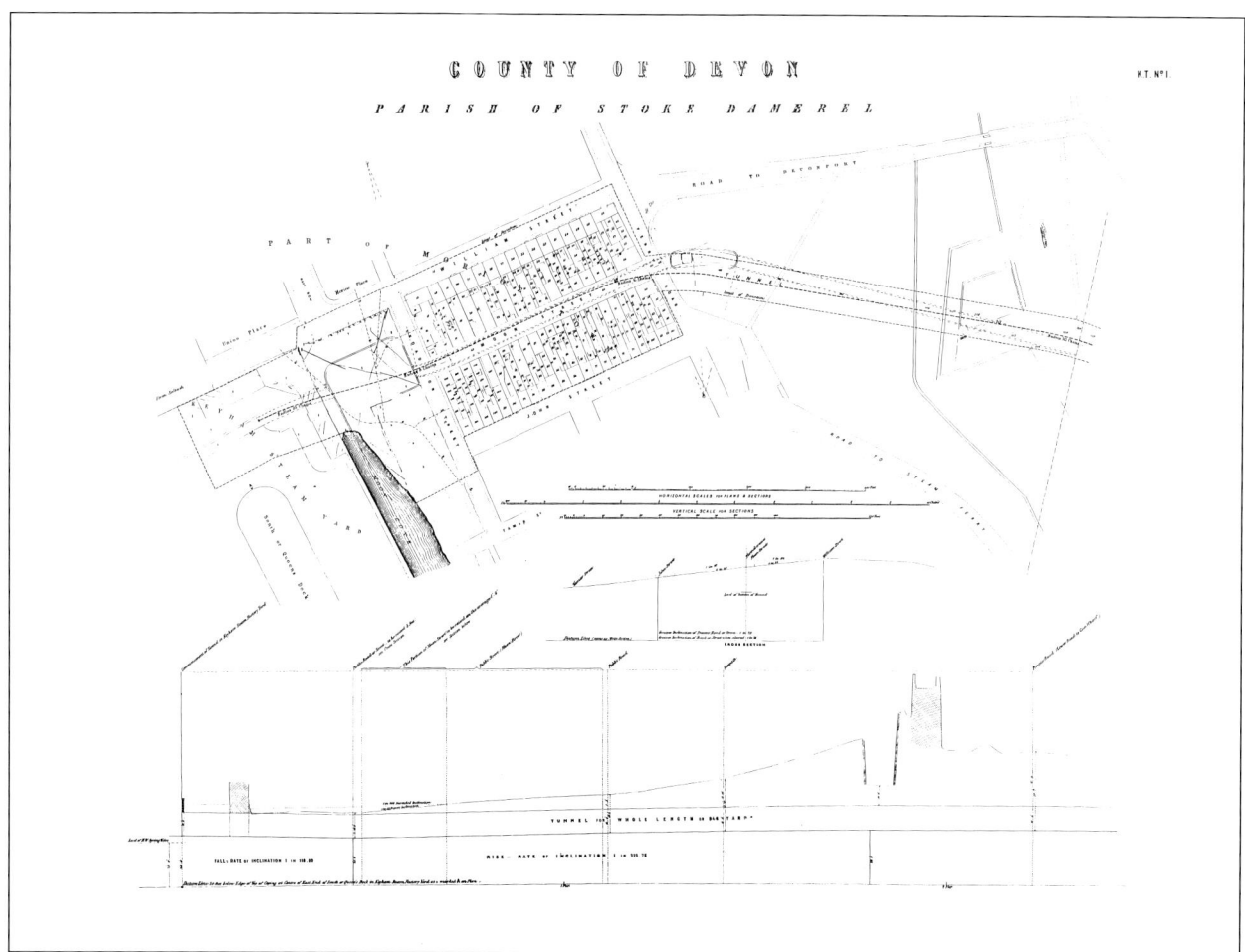

tunnel entrance, was not to be filled in without the written permission of the Admiralty Commissioners. Supplies from the Devonport Gas and Coke Company were to be maintained, at a penalty of ten shillings per hour of interruption.

To assist with planning, six boreholes were sunk to determine the level of rock along the proposed course of the tunnel. The plans were drawn up by a Mr Dament, who was a Plymouth architect who carried on the practice earlier started by Foulston, the designer of many great Plymouth buildings. However, some of the details were to be left to the engineer, as notations indicate that 'Shaft No 1 may not be required and not to be provided except found to be absolutely necessary'. Also at the point adjacent to the access road to the Torpoint Ferry a sharp curve was planned, in the tunnel, and here there was an option for a short open cutting or shaft. The latter was eventually constructed (and later filled in).

Where the tunnel passed outside the Admiralty boundary in Morice Town, property and land in the ownership of the Trustees of the late Sir John St Aubyn were purchased for the sum of £4017.6s.7d. At each intersection of a boundary a marker stone was erected. Fourteen of these boundary marker stones were put up where the tunnel limits passed under the Dockyard walls. To this day at least five of these remain to be seen in the walls of the Dockyard in Morice Town.

The original Engineer, or Superintending Officer, appointed by the Admiralty to oversee the works was Mr J. MacDonnell, who

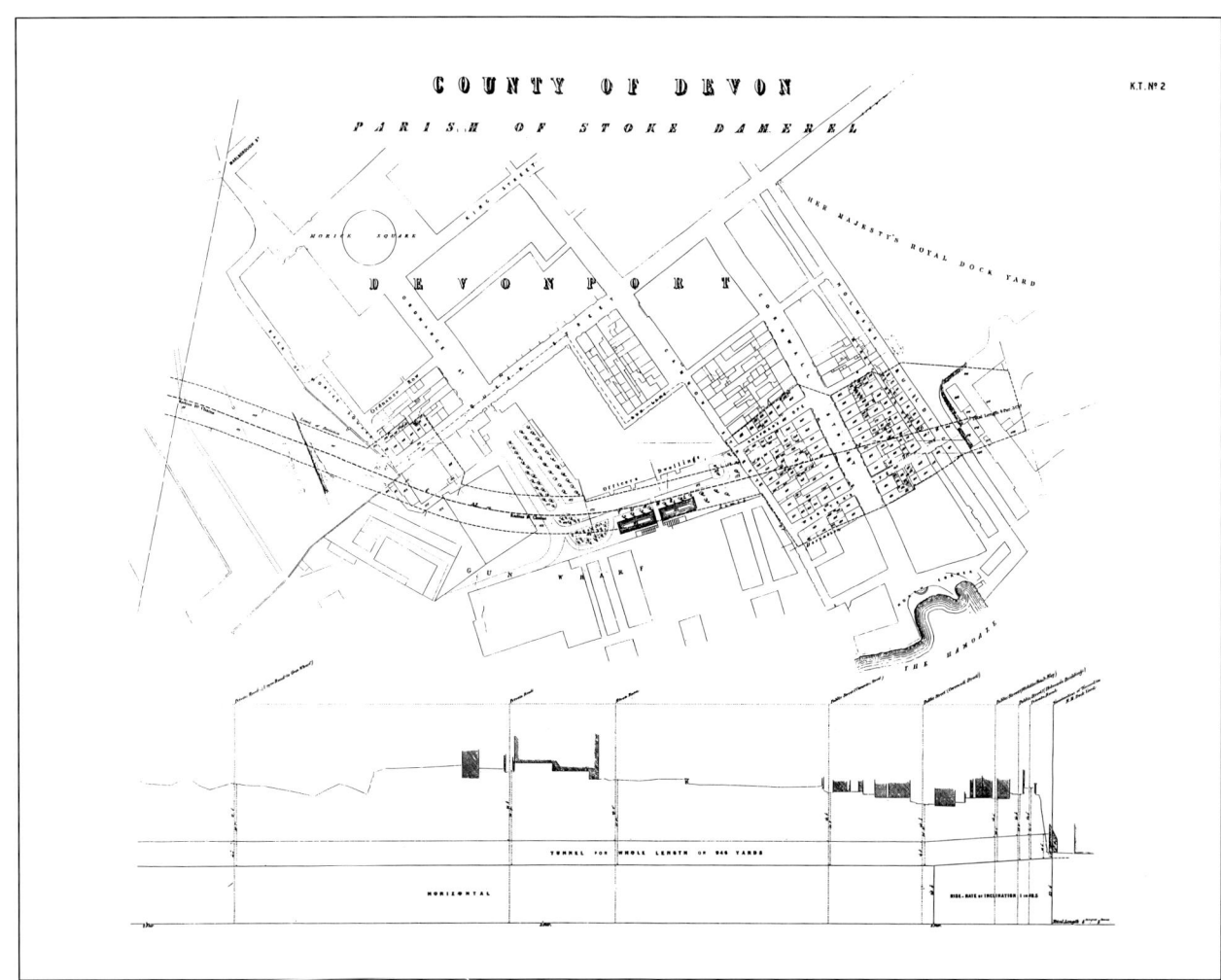

Tunnel Act plans

was succeeded in November 1856 by a Mr Hoppen. They supervised the contractor, Messrs Smith of Woolwich. Construction commenced in April 1855 and up to 270 men were employed. Some kind of temporary tramway was used to haul the spoil out of the bore to waiting barges in the river. It was then taken across the Tamar to Millbrook where it was dumped in a creek. The contractor, however, found some difficulty with the ground as some extra brickwork is recorded in the crown of the arch near one of the air shafts. At the rear of Gun Wharf a cutting of 68 yards was made, over which an existing sewer was carried in a brick arch. At the time of building, there was no access to the Ordnance Depot here; this was to follow in about 1862.

A fairly uneventful period of construction ensued, and completion was effected certainly by April 1857. On pay day Friday 3 April 1857 the workmen of Keyham walked through the tunnel to collect their wages from the pay office in Devonport Yard. Important visitors, such as the Lords of the Admiralty who walked through on the afternoon of Saturday 20 April 1867, had the tunnel shown off to them. But at this time the railway had yet to be laid through from each Yard.

The reason that the Act of Parliament was specific about footpaths in Moon Street was that the tunnel construction here was to be by the cut and cover method. This was used as the tunnel was very close to the surface and involved opening up a trench in the ground the width of the tunnel, building the brickwork lining and filling back with soil. As this was down the middle of a street of houses it is perhaps understandable that the drawings include the note ... 'the works will be executed to the convenience of the occupants of houses on both sides of the Street ... and the method is to be adopted avoiding inconvenience to the occupants', although how this could have been put into practice is less easy to understand, as the tunnel construction occupied the whole width of the roadway.

Acts of Parliament for works such as railways, tunnels, etc., all allow for some minor changes of course, and this is called 'limits of deviation'. The Keyham tunnel was no exception, and an alteration was made to the line of the tunnel under Ferry Road. This allowed the tunnel to follow Moon Street for its full length and then describe a very sharp curve of 216 feet radius, instead of curving at a gentler radius but causing the demolition of a number of buildings at the corner of Moon Street and Ferry Road.

A requirement of the 1854 Act of Parliament for the tunnel was the marking of the tunnel limits at the Yard boundaries. Still located in the perimeter walls are these two marker stones. P. BURKHALTER

THE TUNNEL

The junction to Morice Yard (formerly Gun Wharf) in 1968. On the right is the gated entrance to indicate the original separate 'ownership' of this area. The arch over the track leading south carried the sewer from Devonport. PLYMOUTH NAVAL BASE MUSEUM

Indeed quite a few variances from the approved plans can be noted, even down to such basics as the gradients, as a detailed survey undertaken in 1945 showed when compared with the original plans.

The tunnel is neither level nor straight. From the north portal it drops at 1 in 86 to a low point, 800 feet away, of 8.10 feet above Ordnance Datum. The sharp curve referred to earlier was on a rising gradient of 1 in 188 and from there to the southern portal the upward incline is 1 in 241.

In actual fact the tunnel was in three sections. The most northerly was under the entrance gate-house to Keyham Yard, which was demolished to make way for the 1970's Frigate Complex. This section is some 70 feet long and still exists even though the superstructure of the gatehouse has now gone. Then an open section across James's Yard past some coal vaults, after which was the tunnel proper. South Yard is 2,580 feet further south. In the main section of tunnel were five air shafts to the surface, one of which has since been closed in.

One of the air shafts was relatively shallow as it descended from the bottom of the ditch fortification that ran around the original Devonport Yard. This gave rise to great concern for the Dockyard Police Force. A letter to the Admiralty dated 20 March 1858 calls for extra staff to patrol the tunnel because it was feared that stores could be thrown out of the tunnel and hence into civilian hands. In the same letter other problems to be dealt with by the same proposed patrol were seamen getting over the wall into the Coal Yard at the Keyham end, and disorderly and riotous conduct of workmen whilst proceeding between the Yards.

Just south of the centre point of the tunnel is a long cutting, which today allows access at Morice Yard, and which has had an interesting existence. Originally it was an open cutting in the hill to the rear of, and remote from, Gun Wharf (now Morice Yard). Over this was installed a brick arch carrying the sewer from the Marlborough Street area of Devonport. The cutting was connected to Gun Wharf by a westward cut provided by 1862 for foot and cart traffic only. In 1866, prior to any railway being installed, the main cutting between the tunnel portals was

13

extended northwards by opening up the tunnel for 104 feet to allow for a future rail curve into the Wharf. Part of the major extensions to Gun Wharf of this period was to cut back the hill towards the cutting. To show that the ownership of the Gun Wharf was in different hands (i.e. the Army), a wall and gateway were erected and they still stand today.

When the tunnel was finished a separate contractor, working directly for the Admiralty, laid the floor with an asphalt covering on a concrete base, with granite setts in the centre to take the wear of horses' hooves. Due to the low level of the floor high tides caused flooding problems until later reconstruction improved the drainage.

However the one aspect which was to later make the whole Dockyard Railway unique was that the tunnel was only twelve feet high.

When first opened in 1857, there was no railway through the tunnel, so the floor was laid for cart traffic.

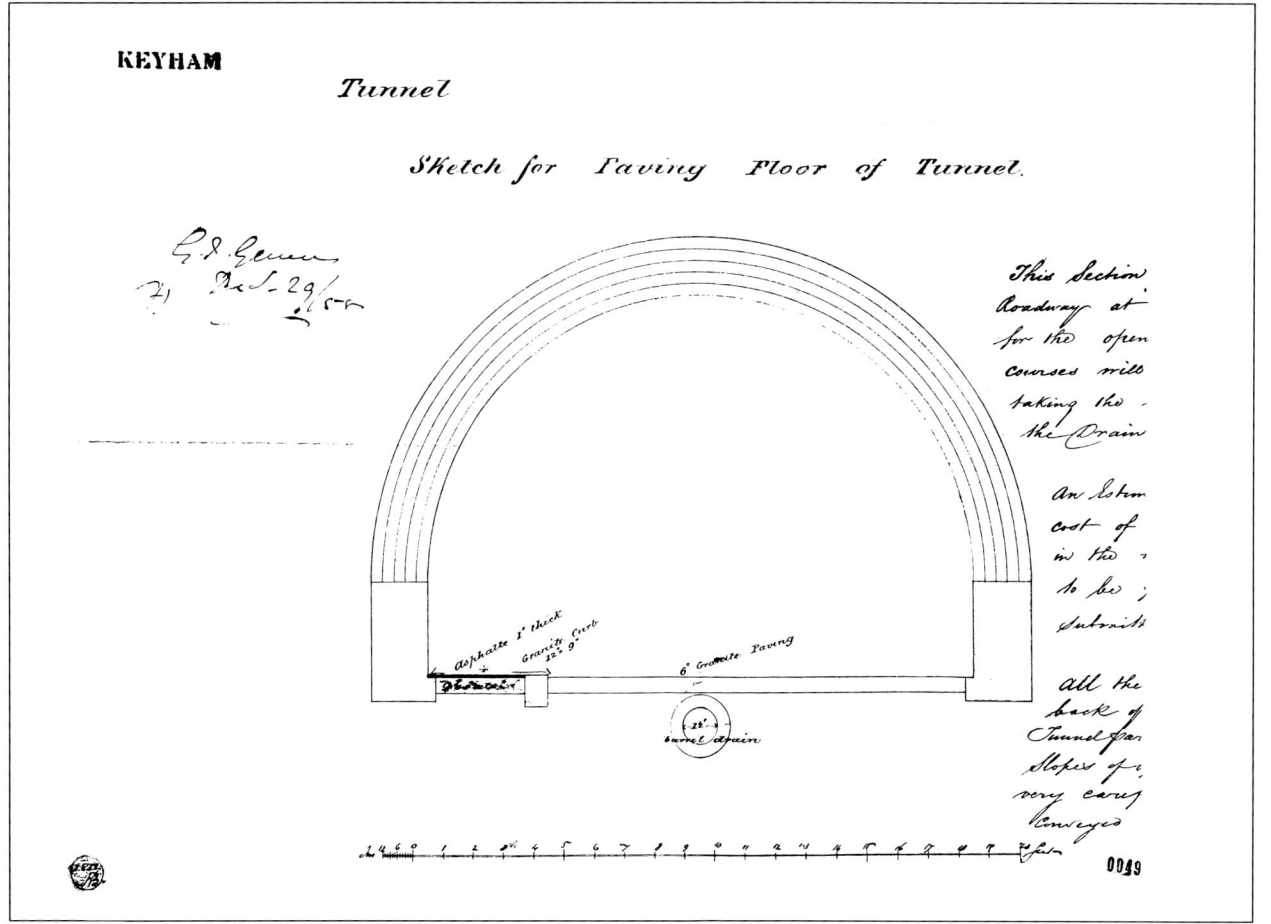

CHAPTER THREE
FIRST RAILWAYS IN THE DOCKYARD

Installations were constructed at Gun Wharf between 1720 and 1724, which form the core of the present buildings in Morice Yard (its current title). These were undertaken by the Board of Ordnance, the separate Government department which handled all of the military's armaments until the Crimean war. The reason for their location here was to serve the Navy at Devonport.

Two substantial storehouses, still in daily use, face each other immediately adjacent to the wharf itself, originally on a line of river frontage much further inland than now. William Cowley, a London stonemason, was contracted for most of the work and he was later joined by Abraham Curtis, a carpenter and joiner. It is recorded that in November 1724 Curtis was paid £6.17s.9d. for '551 feet running of fir quarter 3½ by 2½ inches planed and spiked to the floor for truckways'.

As early as 1817 an extraordinarily detailed proposition for railroads in Devonport Yard was put to the Admiralty. One James Mitchell wrote from His Majesty's Dockyard, Plymouth, on 12 September 1817 to Commissioner Shield, and it is worth quoting the opening part of his report in full:

> Sir,
>
> I beg leave to submit for your consideration the outline of a plan to reduce the expense of transporting timber, stone, etc., from one part of the yard to another and to facilitate the operation, by the introduction of iron railings, whereby the use of horses may be suspended, viz to lay these railways on all the roads excepting that leading from the end of the tap house upwards, two on this to communicate with the place appropriated for storing lots of old timber, and three on the roads in the area of the stockhouses, docksides and sawpits, and two on all the secondary roads. To lay one railway through each smithery to connect with others leading to the anchor racks and chain stacks. To lay a sufficient number of them on the mast and boat slips. To provide suitable means of turning off, and changing from one railway to another, for the purpose of carriages either helping each other, or turning in different directions.
>
> To provided carriages adapted to the railings and of such construction that labourers may transport stores and artefacts their materials with facility.
>
> The whole of single double and triple railways which are here proposed to be laid, on all the roads in the Dockyard, on which stores of any description are transported, if drawn out into a single line of one railway, would be 18,040 yards, or two miles one quarter. Each yard of railing would weigh about 84lb, the total weight of the whole line would be 676 tons, which at £16 per ton is £10,816 a sufficient number of suitable carriages and apparatus may be estimated at £1,200 making a total of £12,016 a sum of little comparative amount in my opinion when the savings and facilities supposed to be affected by this scheme are taken into consideration.

Where it all began. Out of the, now closed, arch at the west end of the Boiler Shop emerged the first broad gauge tramway, laid in 1860. P. BURKHALTER

A number of paragraphs follow expounding the great benefits which would accrue to the Dockyard by adopting the proposal. The Master Shipwright and the Commissioners agreed that the scheme was a good one, and all was set for a revolutionary and far-sighted early use of new technology. But on 16 October came the death knell of the idea. For some reason the matter had been referred by the Navy Board to Portsmouth Yard. Simon Goodrich of that Yard wrote in a report 'that railways were only suitable for quarries or canal building'.

The first tramway in Keyham Yard was laid in 1860, for on 7 March of that year 6,750 feet of rails were ordered from Ebbw Vale at £10 per ton. A single line of rails laid to the broad gauge of 7 feet 0¼ inches ran from the Boiler Shop on the northern side of the Quadrangle, along the east of North Basin (now No 3 basin) to the 20 ton crane in the north-east corner of South Basin (now No 2 basin). An interesting report, dated 30 December 1859, exists on the use of Taylor traction engines. Here the usefulness of the machine is extensively examined, and future developments are outlined to propose that larger and broader wheels be fitted 'with a groove in the periphery to allow use on the present railroads at Keyham which are of the broad gauge or 7 feet 2in from centre to centre'. Confusingly this would seem to indicate an earlier date for the laying of rails.

Further lines of a tramway system were laid in Keyham Yard into and around the Quadrangle between 1862 and 1865. Plans which accompany the 1865 Agreement with the Cornwall Railway show one and a quarter miles of tracks, with one turntable on the east side of the North Basin to give access into the centre of the Quadrangle. Proposed lines are also indicated, but none to the tunnel. Trucks drawn by two horses hauled iron plating to the hydraulic press.

Work was undertaken at this time to complete the northern quay of North Basin, which had really only had its southern side properly built. From 1865 to at least 1867 a contractor called W. Jackson was employed by the Admiralty to extend the size of the basin by nearly 400 feet, north to south, and the depth from 34 feet to 40 feet. At the northern wall provision was made for a new entrance to any further basin to the north. The contractor utilised a standard gauge railway to assist in his task, for which he had purchased an Aveling & Porter locomotive. The spoil from this job was being tipped in Keyham Lake. This would appear to be the first use of a purpose built railway locomotive in the Yards.

In Gun Wharf, a major programme of extensions was implemented in the mid 1860s. A detailed description of the progress in April 1867 gives an indication of the scale of the work and the improvements effected. Hitherto the boundary of the Ordnance Depot had been the wall of the fortifications surrounding Devonport Yard. With the construction of Keyham Yard, this had become somewhat redundant. Therefore the opportunity was taken to extend the Gun Wharf facility, and in the course of this the wall was demolished. The extension is the area now up to New Passage Hill and Ferry Road, with the old fortifications gateway re-erected at its north-east corner, where it stands today. The hill was dug into and two levels created, and a new road built from the gateway down to the old buildings.

As part of the permanent works tramways were laid to move heavy stores between the wharf on the river and the various buildings. The intriguing aspect of this is that two gauges were installed, 18 inch and 7 feet 0¼ inch. The narrow gauge served the Sub-Marine Mining Establishment, linking the workshops and torpedo store to the Camber adjacent to the Torpoint Ferry. The broad gauge lines enabled stores unloaded by the river wharf steam cranes to be carried to the factory buildings, and coal to the boiler house near to the tunnel entrance, via a turntable.

The April 1867 report mentioned above noted that the tunnel had no railway within it, but that it was 'shortly [to] be accomplished'. It also noted that the open cutting had been arranged to allow a line of rails to turn off into the Gun Wharf, although two years

1862 Yard Plan

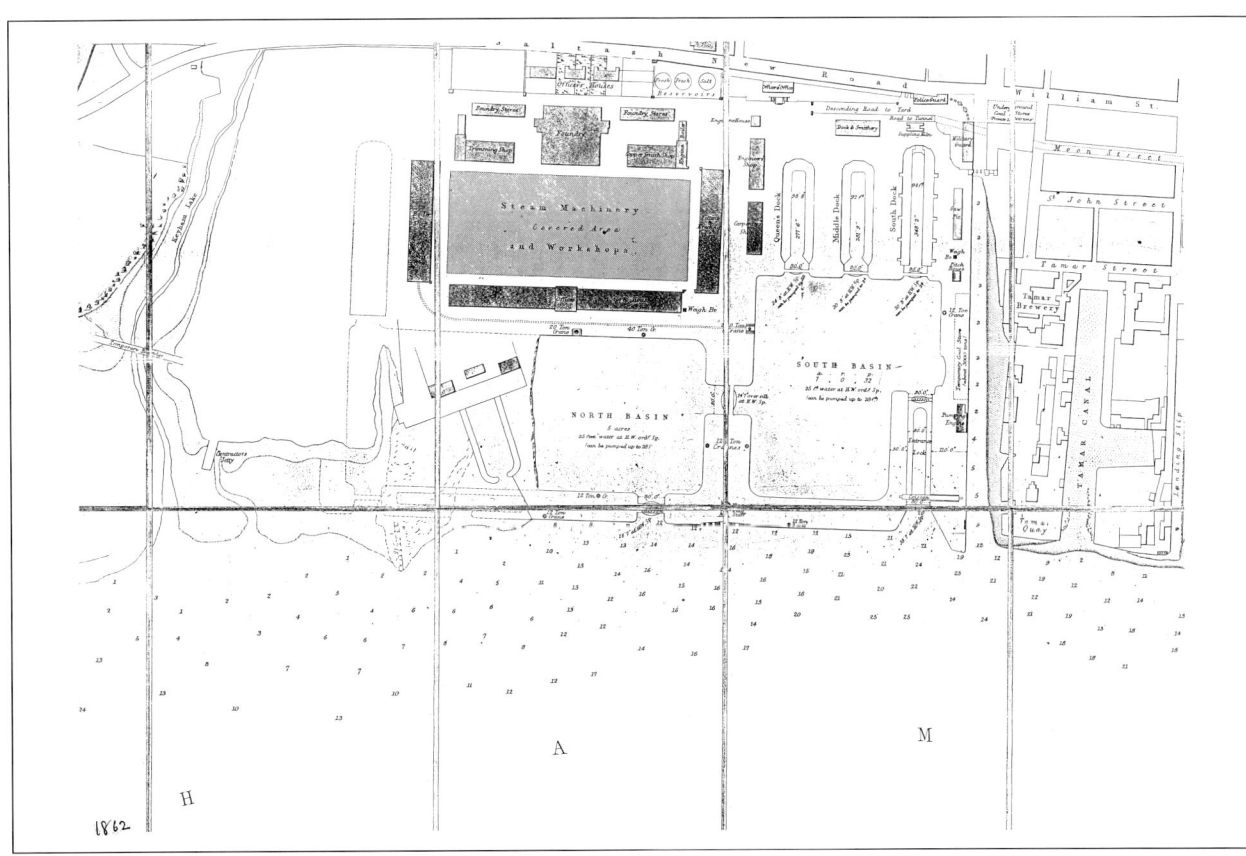

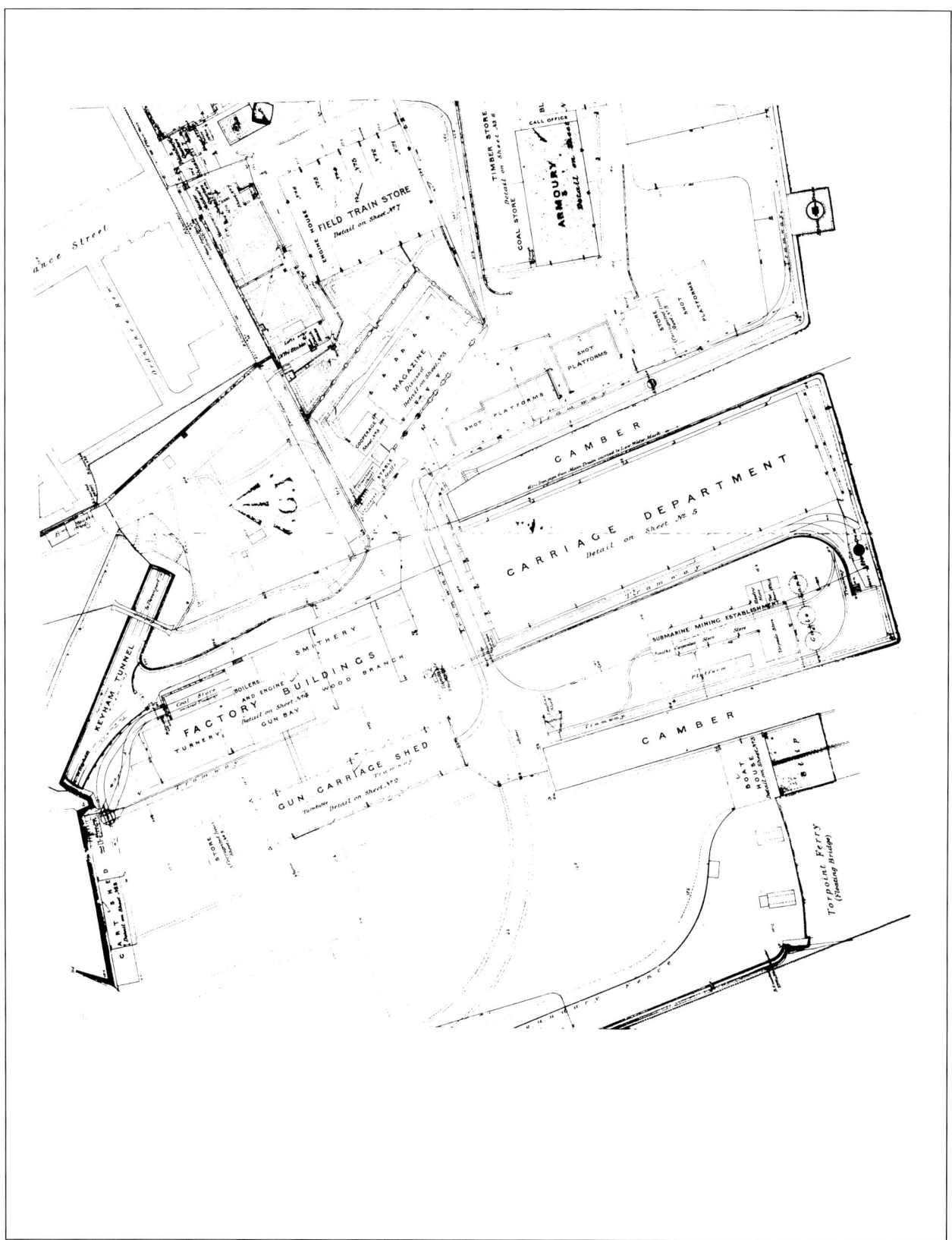

Gun Wharf showing broad gauge and narrow gauge railways after the enlargement works in 1867

earlier it was considered that a turntable be installed with tracks for access at a cost of £2,015.15s.10d. A record drawing dated 3 June 1880 shows the standard gauge in the cutting between the tunnels, with the rails ready to connect to the Gun Wharf, but the broad gauge within the Wharf area still in existence. A contract was advertised in January 1882 for railway extensions in the Gun Wharf, under the jurisdiction of the District Royal Engineers Office, which would indicate the replacement of the broad gauge with standard to allow interchange with the remainder of the Devonport lines, via the tunnel.

During the tenure of Rear Admiral the Hon. J. R. Drummond as Admiral Superintendent (1866-70), a tramway incline was installed at a cost of £2,000 immediately adjacent to the tunnel entrance in Devonport Yard. A 30 h.p. steam engine hauled carts on the 1 in 5 incline, until the Admiral's wife objected to the noise right next to their residence. The Admiralty acquired its first locomotive in March 1869, an Aveling & Porter, perhaps influenced by the contractor W. Jackson's use of one from this manufacturer at that time. Avelings had offered the loan of one of their products for three months trial when sending the Dockyard Engineer a page from their catalogue.

Other works which necessitated use of temporary railways was the re-construction of No 3 Dock in Devonport Yard. This was started in 1876, but was beset with all sorts of difficulties until final completion in 1882. The sides fell in, storms damaged the coffer dam, excavations collapsed, and when complete it could not be used as no capstans had been installed. Extensive horse-worked wagon-ways were laid down in the bottom of the works, by the contractor Mr J. Pethick, of Norley Buildings, Plymouth, with a rope-hauled incline to ferry loads to and from ground level.

The Aveling & Porter engine was the stalwart of the Dockyard system until the 1880s. The next locomotives to be acquired for here are a little uncertain, but could have been in 1880 and in 1884 when the Admiralty may have bought engines from Hughes and Falcon Engine Co., respectively.

The Dockyard was again in the marketplace for motive-power in the closing years of the nineteenth century, and in January 1897 had John Fowler & Co. deliver their works No 7710. Two years later Messrs Hawthorn Leslie & Co. delivered in February of 1899 two locomotives to become Dockyard numbers 1 and 2.

In c. 1867 a short lived rail incline was installed to lower materials into South Yard, the assumed site is shown here in September 1992.
P. BURKHALTER

The troubled enlargement of 3 Dock in June 1879 by the local contractor, J Pethick. Temporary railways are in evidence with an inclined plane access on the left. The river caisson is in the distance. Note the horse for haulage on the dock floor. PUBLIC RECORD OFFICE ADM195/60

Looking in the opposite direction, and one year on. Clearly seen at ground level is the (then) recently altered south smithery with the arch of the railway opening leading to the tunnel. PUBLIC RECORD OFFICE ADM195/60

CHAPTER FOUR

CONNECTION TO THE CORNWALL RAILWAY

With the impending arrival of the South Devon Railway in Plymouth in May 1848 proposals were made to extend the line westwards into Cornwall. The first engineer laid out the line to include a train ferry across the Hamoaze to Torpoint, and this proposed route appears on some contemporary maps of Plymouth. However, I. K. Brunel was later appointed as engineer and designed a new route to include a high level bridge to Saltash.

Work started in Cornwall in 1847 but the depression after the first Railway Mania caused work to be suspended for three years. After re-starting progress was slow, with construction of the line on the Devon side commencing in 1853. The connection with the SDR was to be just north of Millbay Station but it was not until 1858 before the broad gauge rails were installed from here to the new Saltash Bridge. The Cornwall Railway line throughout to Truro opened on

Original manuscript of agreement between the Cornwall Railway and the Admiralty

4 May 1859. The only station between Millbay and Saltash was at Devonport on the hillside overlooking the entrance to Keyham Steam Yard.

The benefit of a connection to this new mode of transportation was not lost on the Admiralty. Before the Cornwall Railway opened the Keyham Yard Civil Engineer had surveyed the ground and submitted a preliminary favourable report on 9 April 1859. At the Cornwall Railway Board meeting held on 21 April 1859 at Liskeard, the last before the opening of the line, a letter was read from the Admiralty Engineer at Keyham Yard, which proposed a railway connection to the Cornwall Railway's line near Weston Mill Creek. The Yard Engineer's final report of 21 May set down various methods to achieve a connection. Mr Woollcombe (the acting Chairman of the Cornwall Railway, and also Town Clerk of Devonport) subsequently looked over the site of the proposed branch and an apparent positive approach was taken at the subsequent Board meeting in May. The Admiralty purchased the land for the line on 20 March 1862, and in December 1864 Mr Woollcombe met with Mr Townsend, the Superintending Engineer of Keyham Yard, which resulted in agreement to proceed with the branch construction. A draft agreement with the Admiralty authorities was reported to the Board on 20 October 1865. As the line was constructed entirely on private land, and not intended for public use, no Act of Parliament was necessary. It was estimated that the works would cost £8,355.10s.8d, and in anticipation of the formal signing of this document, a contract was let to a Mr William Drew for the earthworks, masonry, ballast and fencing. Rails were obtained from the Rhymney Iron Co. for £7.10s.0d delivered to Plymouth. The final agreement was drawn up and confirmed at the Cornwall Railway Board meeting on 15 December 1865, which date it bore. It is the only known legal document relating to the connection between the Dockyard lines and the main line, hence could be said to be still in force to this day.

Simply put it is the Cornwall Railway Company, which entered into an agreement with (less simply) 'The Commissioners for Executing the Office of Lord High Admiral of the United Kingdom of Great Britain and Ireland for and on behalf of Her Majesty her heirs and successors'.

Twenty conditions follow, which:

> Committed the Cornwall Railway to build a single line of broad gauge railway from a point near the eastern end of Weston Mill viaduct (which is in fact nearly on a north to south alignment), to include a siding and turnouts and turntables.
>
> Required the Admiralty to pay interest at the rate of 4% on the value of work done during construction.
>
> Upon completion the Cornwall Railway was to receive an annuity of £332.4s.0d, paid half yearly.
>
> Allow the Cornwall Railway to execute additional works should the Admiralty direct, and pay for at cost.
>
> The Cornwall Railway was to maintain the new, and existing, railways in the Dockyard.
>
> The Admiralty was to pay the cost of all signals and switches, and of the men to operate them.
>
> If required by the Dockyard, the Cornwall Railway was to provide engines for shunting around the lines, and for which the Yard was to pay the same rate as the Cornwall Railway paid their locomotive contractor. The South Devon Railway was contracted to provide all locomotive power, including crews, on the Cornwall Railway.
>
> A number of conditions related to the resolution of disputes, should they arise.

The agreement was signed for the Cornwall Company by Robert Tweedy, the Chairman.

The arrangement for the CR to provide engines for shunting only lasted until the Admiralty purchased a locomotive in March 1869.

Accompanying the Agreement were the plans, sections and specifications. The length of the new line was to be 5 furlongs $9^1/_2$ chains, and the height difference $38^1/_2$ feet. A short level section at the junction end led to a descent of 1 in 78, then 1 in 67. Two cuttings with a greatest depth of 21 feet were complimented by a short embankment 14 feet high. The specification in full follows:-

> Specification of Work to be performed in constructing a line of Railway from the Cornwall Railway, at a point near the eastern end of Weston Mill Viaduct, to Keyham Dock Yard, a distance of Six Furlongs.
>
> The Government to find land and give possession when required.
>
> The works to be carried out as shown on Plan Sections, submitted by the Cornwall Railway Company, which are based upon information conveyed by plans and sections, produced by the Government. The line to be single line of rails, with a siding at or near the Junction with the Cornwall Railway and to be protected with the usual Junction Signals
>
> Earthwork
>
> The Cuttings and Embankments to be formed as shown by Cross Sections on plan, except when the Rock in Cutting shall be considered sufficiently solid to stand at a less slope, in which case the contracting parties, shall not be asked to cut it back to the slope shown.
>
> The soil on the site of Cuttings to be deposited at such points, as may be selected on the higher side of the line, between it and the Saltash Turnpike Road.
>
> The excavation in excess of what is required to form embankments, to be deposited at the nearest convenient point alongside of the filling at present in progress from the Basin being formed in Keyham Yard. If taken to the sea edge of present filling, it shall be deposited parallel with the existing water line, but at the nearest point to the respective cuttings.
>
> Ballast
>
> The line shall be properly Ballasted with one foot of coarsely broken stone of the hardest description produced from the cuttings, covered with six inches of finely broken stone or gravel similar in all respects to that used on the Cornwall Railway.
>
> Fencing
>
> The Fencing to be ordinary Post and Rail Fence, similar in all respects to that used on the Cornwall Railway.
>
> Masonry
>
> The Masonry in Abutments of Keyham Lake Bridge and retaining Wall, in Cutting near Bridge built by Government, to be of the same character and of equal quality to the Masonry of that Bridge. The Bridge over Keyham Lake to be constructed with Masonry abutments and wrought Girders of approved construction.
>
> Permanent Way
>
> The Permanent Way to be laid on Transverse Sleepers, with chairs and fastenings similar to those in use on broad gauge Railways with double headed Rails, weighing 72lb per yard; with Switches, Crossings &tc at the Junction with Cornwall Railway and the Siding complete.
>
> If the scheme with Turntable is carried out the Permanent Way to be laid similar to the portion of the Line.
>
> The Turntable shall be Cowan & Sheldon of Carlisle 40 feet diameter. The Bed for Roller Path and coping, limestone ashlar, and the center[sic] pier of large blocks of scabbled limestone. The remainder of the Masonry to be filled rubble built with Limestone. The bottom to be covered with six inches of concrete and the pit properly drained.
>
> (signed) Robt. Tweedy
> Chairman Cornwall Railway'

Having agreed to the Admiralty paying for the work by an annuity, this left the Cornwall Railway without the means to pay for the work themselves. The contractor, Drew, was first asked to accept Bonds in lieu of payment but he refused. Subsequently the railway's bankers agreed to lend £1,000, and Sir W. Williams loaned them a total of £6,800 at 5%, which was eventually paid back in late 1871. Note the disparity between the Admiralty paying 4% and the Cornwall Railway having to borrow the money at 1% higher.

A subsequent agreement dated 1 August 1867 provided for an additional siding to run parallel to the Cornwall Railway main line for a distance of one hundred yards, for the exclusive use of the Dockyard traffic. This was to cost the Admiralty £216. But more importantly it would appear that the original annuity could be redeemed at a cost of £8,571.10s.8d. This was not taken up, and the Admiralty continued paying an Annuity of £410.11s.8d. An exchange of correspondence in 1890 and 1891 between the Admiralty and the GWR established an agreed value of £10,315.3s.11d to redeem the Annuity and purchase the line outright. However it was to be 1903 before this action was taken.

The branch line was completed on 20 June 1867 at a total cost of £6,587.6s.1d. Hopefully the £2,000 'profit' went some way to offset the loss on borrowing.

The original scene at Keyham was very different from today. The Cornwall Railway was single track at this point, and the nearest stations were Devonport and Saltash. The adjacent viaduct was the original Brunel timber structure, crossing a wide expanse of tidal water which receded at low tide to reveal a large area of mud flat. No housing could be seen, and fields extended on all sides, for the Barracks were not to appear until twenty years later. The road running from the Keyham Yard main gate crossed over the Cornwall line here, to descend the hill and join the main road from Plymouth to Saltash Passage. It was a remote place, the junction being located in a rock sided cutting completely out of sight of human habitation.

Even the trackbed was not as now, as Westom Mill Viaduct was some 15 feet lower than today, hence the junction would be equally lower. Gradients of 1 in 61 on the main line descended to the bridge level, which was a typical Cornwall Railway structure over tidal waters of 29 timber trestles, mostly supported on timber piles sunk deep into the mud of the creek.

The Cornwall Railway was being asked in June 1868 to carry out some additional work and lay a short loop on the east side of the North Basin, to include a 13 feet diameter Heanett & Spinks turntable. At the same time a telegraph connection was being proposed between Keyham Yard and Millbay Station, to help in the efficient working of trains.

The limitations of a broad gauge connection only were apparent, for the Admiralty as well as others had to suffer the delays that trans-shipment created where the ultimate destination was on the standard gauge. When the L&SWR and its associated companies planned an extension of the standard gauge to Plymouth the Admiralty was quick to put its case. The first correspondence between the two was exchanged as early as October 1871, and continued in parallel with the Cornwall & West Cornwall Railway Act of 1871, which gave authority for the works and allowed the raising of further capital. Ultimately £200,000 was raised this way to pay for various works including the Dockyard mixed gauge scheme.

The matter of extending the railway through the tunnel into Devonport Yard was also pressing. As early as 1865, at the same time as the main line connection was being planned, Townsend (the Keyham Yard Engineer) was considering the possible layout of tracks in Devonport Yard. A plan survives dated 9 February 1865 which shows a never to be implemented proposal for an extensive broad gauge layout of trackwork in South Yard, including lines which were never installed throughout the life of the railway.

Through 1870 and into 1872, the Cornwall Railway and the Admiralty engaged

Over 100 years since the Great Western Railway dispensed with the Broad Gauge, there still remained this dual gauge wagon turntable in South Yard, relocated here from north-east of 3 Basin in North Yard sometime since the second war. Pictured here in 1992 in situ, it was removed in August 1996 and is preserved on site.
COLLECTION P. BURKHALTER

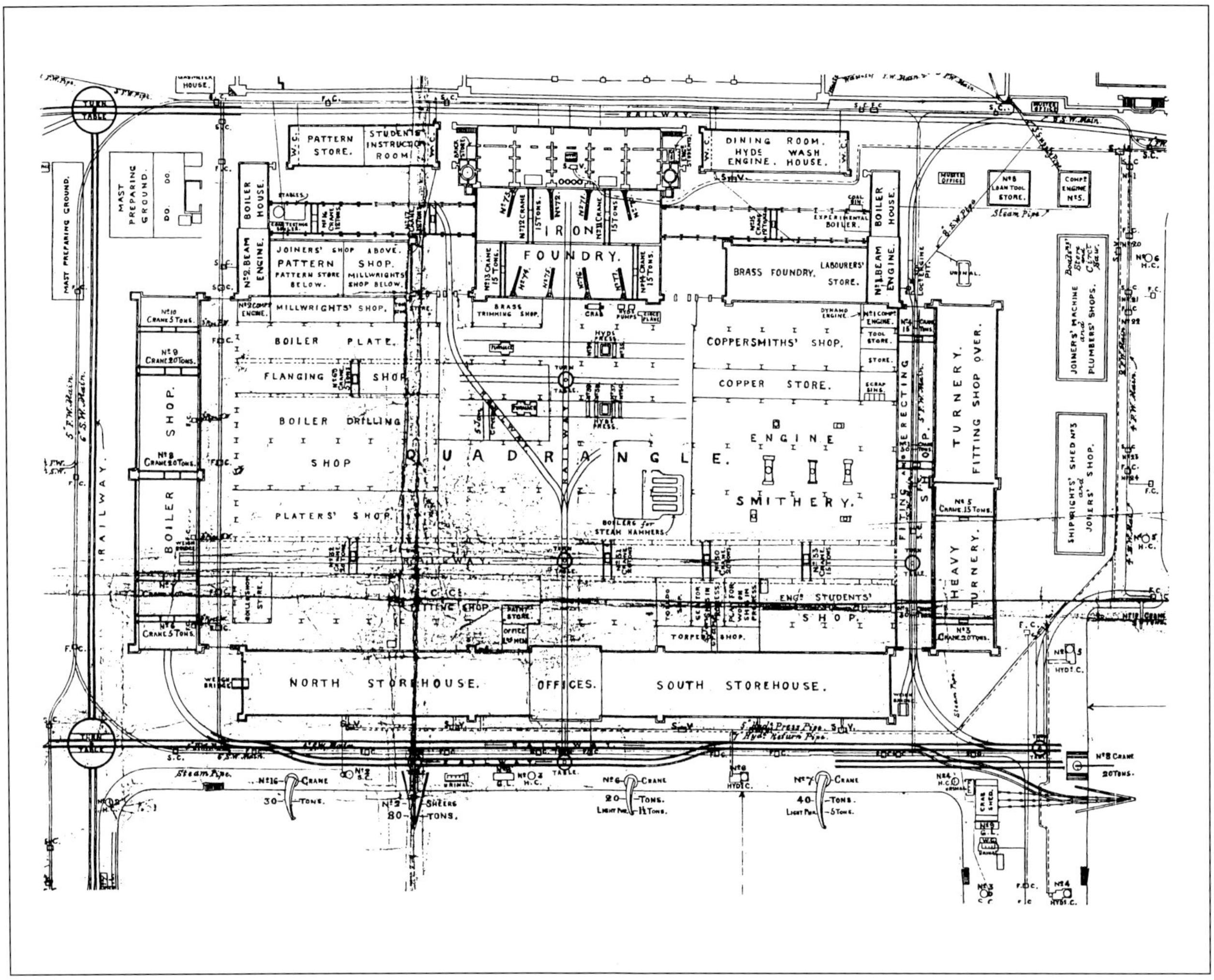

CONNECTION TO THE CORNWALL RAILWAY

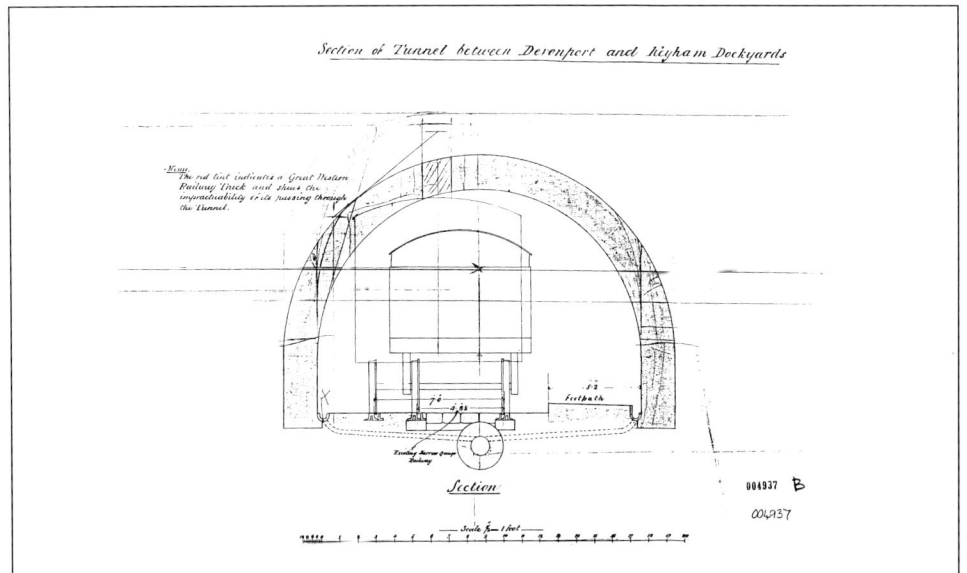

c1880 Quadrangle. Note the dual gauge tracks to the west and north.

c1870 Section through the tunnel with a Broad Gauge truck superimposed to illustrate 'the impracticability of passing through'

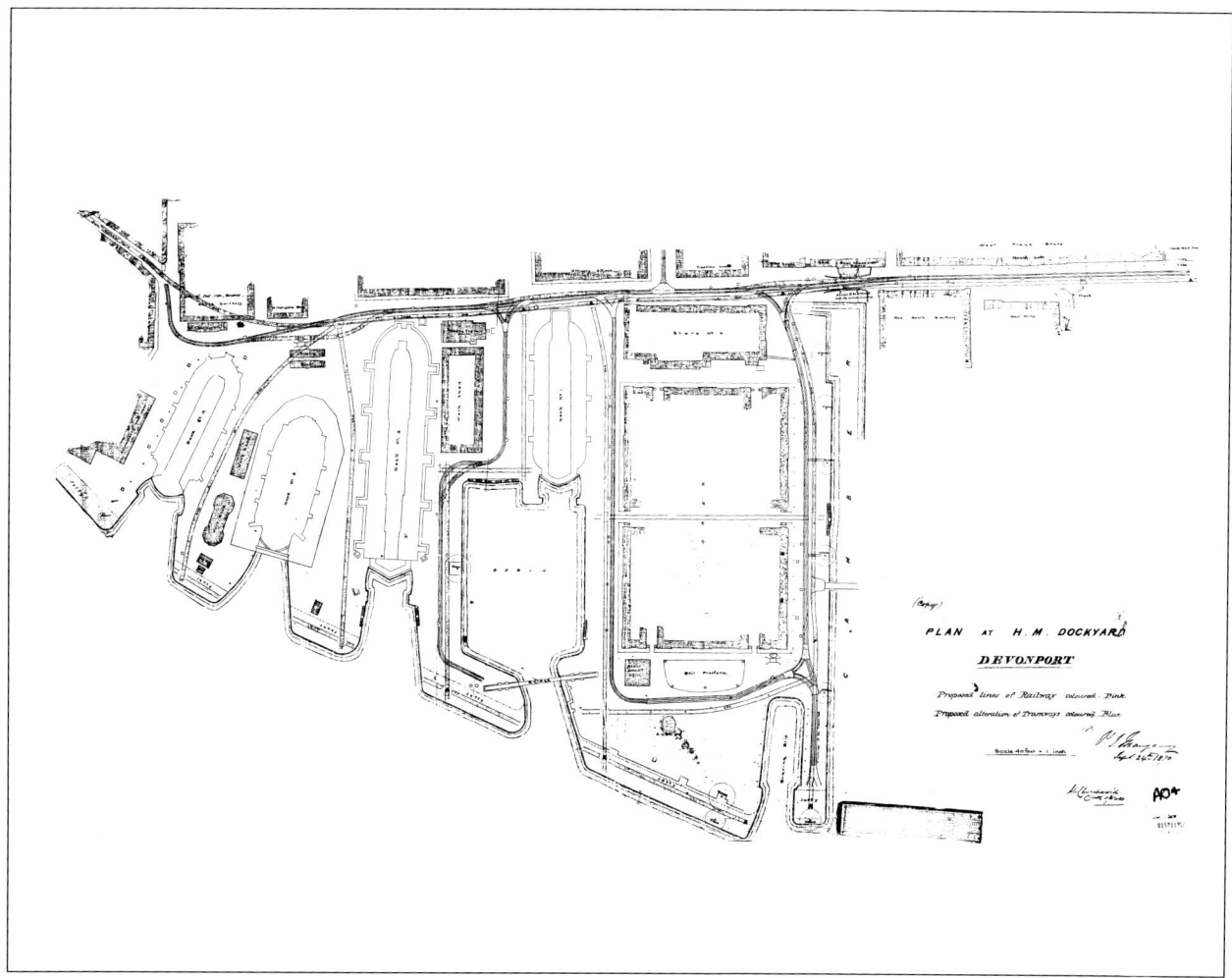

Devonport (now South) Yard showing proposed railways, signed by the Cornwall Railway Engineer, P.J. Margary on 24 September 1870.

in extensive discussion on the matter of the proposed extension of the railway through the tunnel to Devonport Yard. The tone of the correspondence clearly indicates that no rails existed then, so we can deduce that no earlier tramway in the tunnel was present. The plans show some considerable thought to the difficulties of squeezing broad gauge rolling stock into the restricted confines of the tunnel profile, with even a sketch of the crown being cut out upwards into a pointed shape. The Cornwall Railway Engineer, Margary, wanted the tunnel curve eased out, but no doubt the Admiralty were less than enthusiastic at the likely cost. Eventually events overtook the problem and on 24 February 1872 the Cornwall Railway was told that 'My Lord Commissioners' had decided to install standard gauge only. Hence at the Board Meeting on 27 May 1875 Mr Margary was instructed to obtain the necessary materials, when available at favourable prices, for these works.

On 17 May 1876 standard gauge trains finally reached Plymouth via Okehampton, Lydford and the GWR Launceston branch. A new connection, named the Cornwall Loop, bypassed Millbay and allowed the L&SWR direct access into its new terminal at Devonport. The connection to the Dockyard was achieved by laying the third rail on the Cornwall Railway main line to a distance of 10 chains west of Keyham Junction. This end point of standard gauge would have been about half way out on the timber Weston Mill Viaduct. Quite how the rails were ended is not apparent, and no mishaps have been recorded of standard gauge trains running off the end.

CONNECTION TO THE CORNWALL RAILWAY

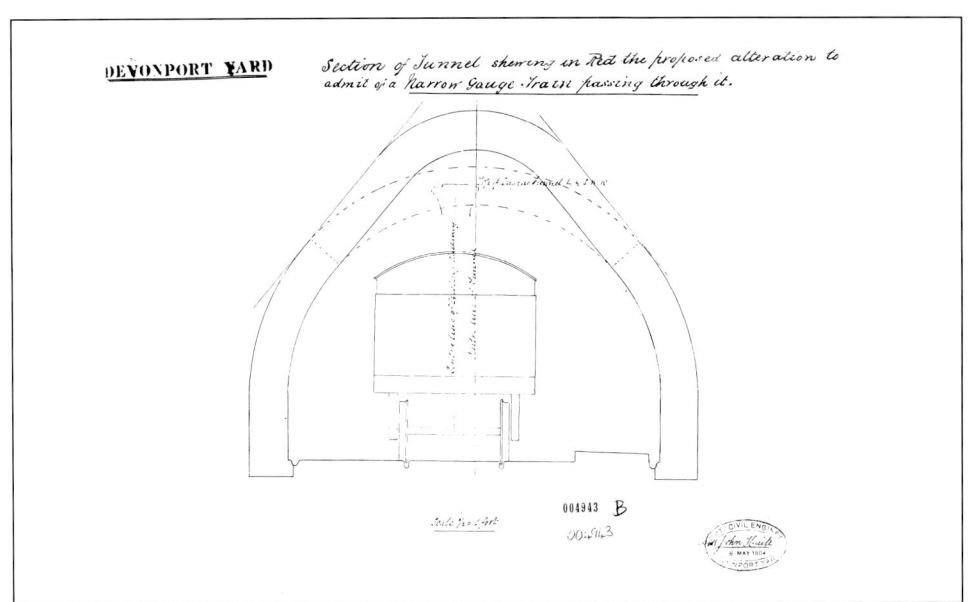

1884 Various investigations of the tunnel clearances (or lack of) for main-line trucks

1879 Cross section of tunnel showing the railway.

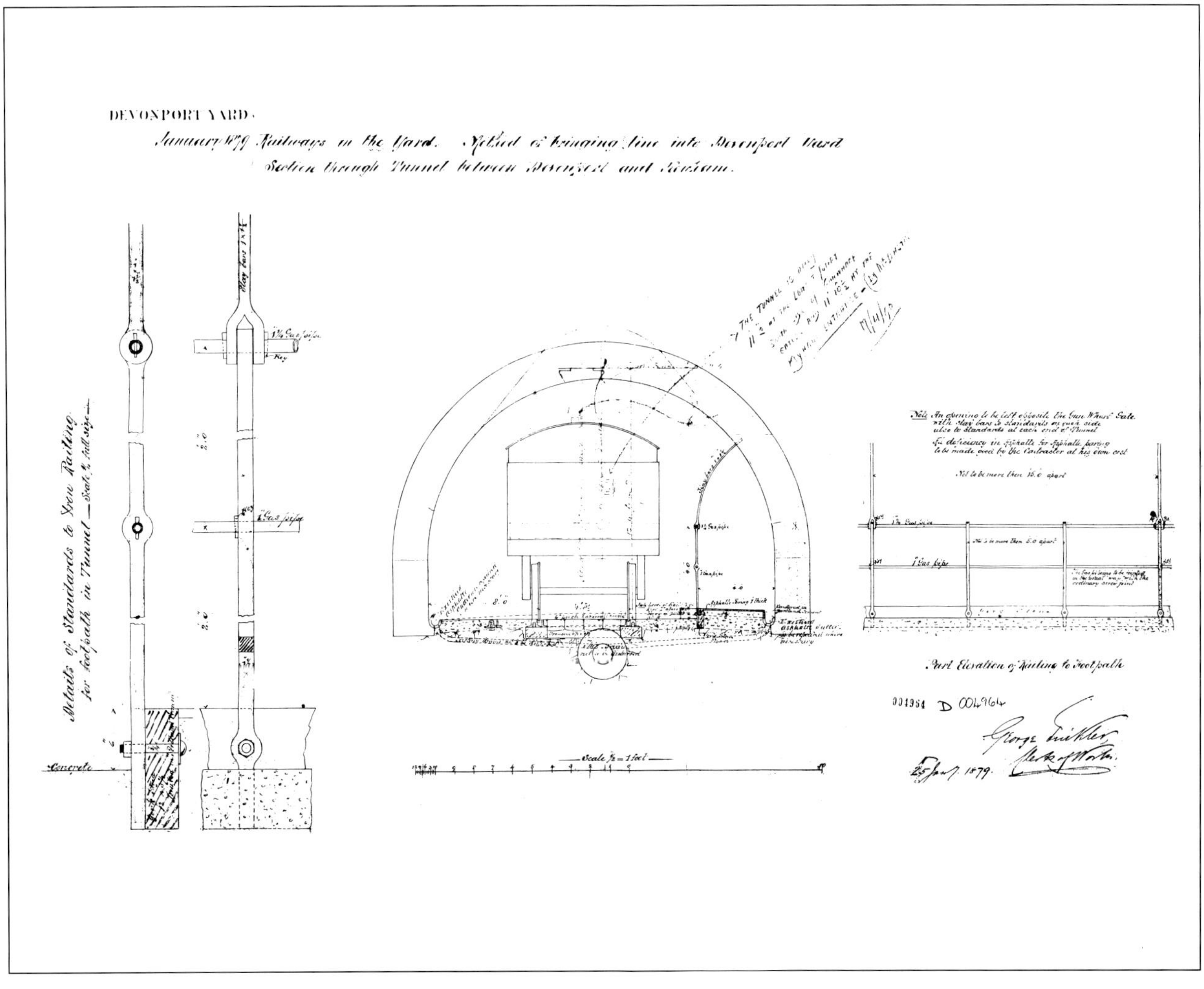

1887 Cross section of trackwork in South Yard.

1879 Standard gauge track in the tunnel

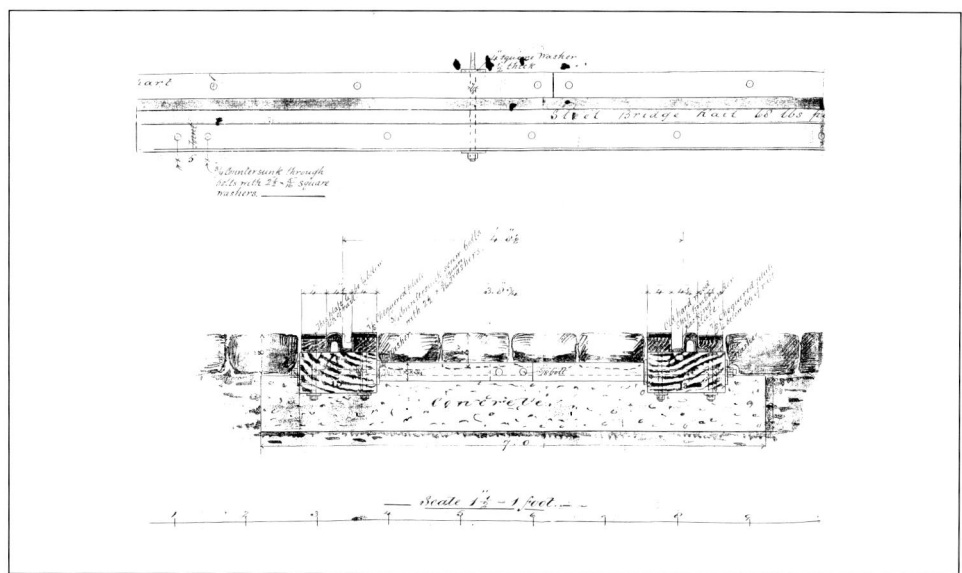

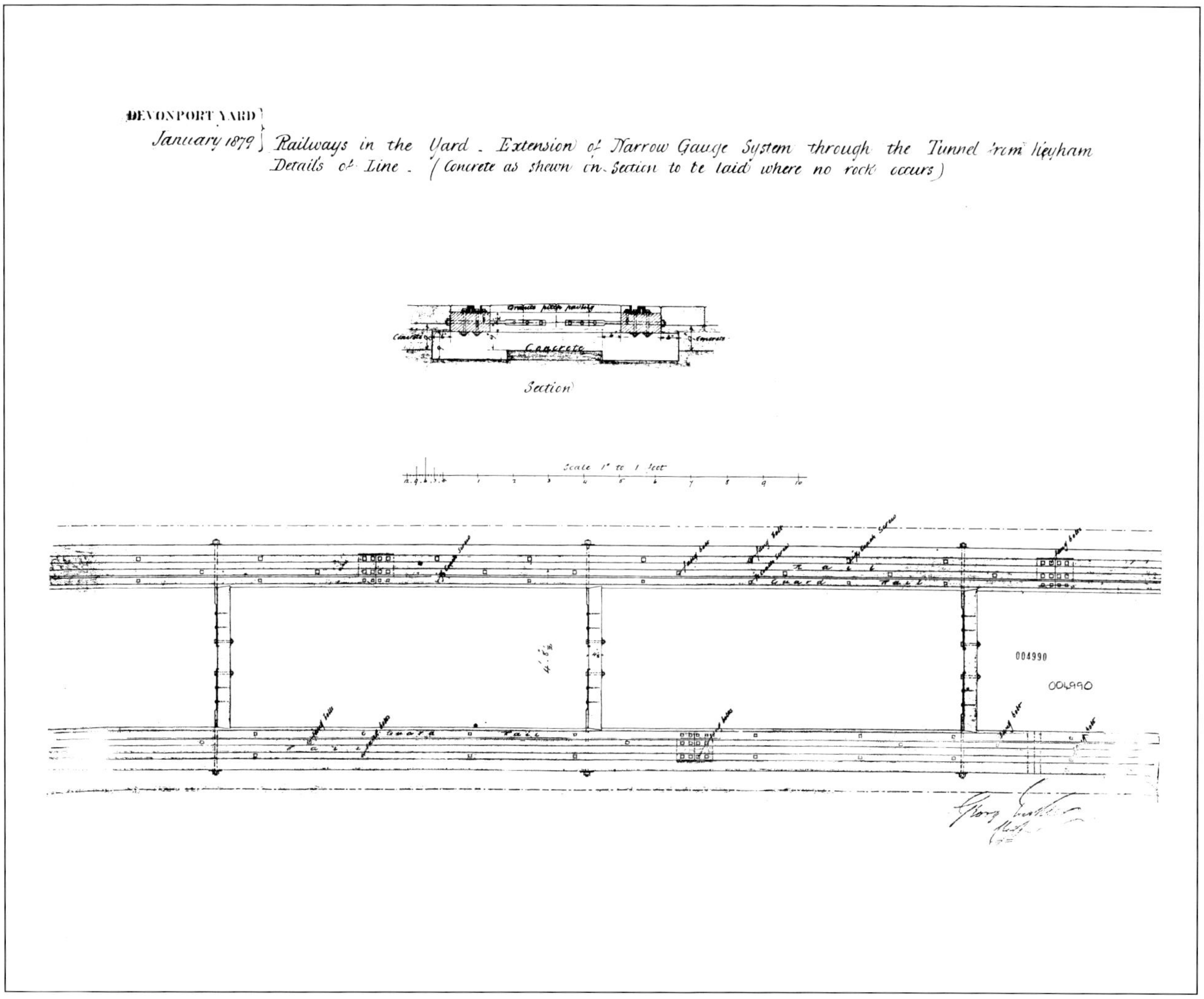

Within the tunnel in 1994, and track is still in situ. On the left is the footway. P. BURKHALTER

The very sharp 216 feet radius curve in the tunnel has always proved troublesome. High on the right are the score marks of loads rather too large. P. BURKHALTER

When the standard gauge railway was constructed in the tunnel by the Cornwall Railway in 1876 to 1877, the arrangements for pedestrians to walk through was continued. To allow this a raised footpath was built on the east side of the new tracks, a facility used to the very end of rail services. Immediately opposite the southern portal of the tunnel in Devonport Yard is located the one of the Yard's smithery buildings. Rather than demolish this building, the Admiralty arranged for replacement furnaces to be installed elsewhere, and the railway passed through the building in a corrugated iron sheet 'tunnel'. This novel layout remained in use for the whole of the life of rail services to South Yard, and this building still stands with the 'tunnel' in-situ.

DEVONPORT DOCKYARD RAILWAY

LEFT: *At the very south of the railway. It ends up against a retaining wall, without ceremony. September 1992.* P. BURKHALTER

BELOW: *Almost at the southern extremity of South Yard, this 1972 view shows internal wagons loaded with timber boards at the sawmills.* COLLECTION P. BURKHALTER

BOTTOM: *Immediately to the north of the Camber in South Yard was a general storage area, on the site of the storehouses destroyed in the blitz. Note the steam crane. c1954.* PLYMOUTH NAVAL BASE MUSEUM

CONNECTION TO THE CORNWALL RAILWAY

TOP: To gain access from the south portal of the tunnel, an existing building had an arch cut through it for the railway. On the left is the signal box.
August 1972. COLLECTION P. BURKHALTER
ABOVE: Squeezed between the rear of the south smithery and the tunnel portal is a roadway, and signals controlled the road traffic over the railway. This view taken ten years after rail traffic ceased, when the signals were still extant, but long defunct. 1992. P. BURKHALTER
RIGHT: No photograph has come to light of the southern portal of the tunnel in railway days. Here the open mouth gapes vacantly in 1992.
DEVONPORT MANAGEMENT LTD.

Looking north into James Yard from the tunnel entrance in September 1951. Ahead is the short curved section that pierced the basement of one of the Albert Gate entrance structures.
HAROLD D BOWTELL

Not explained in any of the surviving instructions are stop signals placed some 100 yards from each portal, and facing inbound trains. Perhaps so placed to give a warning to drivers should the signalman observe a problem with the train as it passes him.
P. BURKHALTER

The turnout to Morice Yard was released by the train staff. In 1992 the lever was still in position, some ten years after the last train. P. BURKHALTER

RIGHT: *At 11.35 on 12 October 1968 the northernmost tunnel portal with the Dockyard clock, that was moved across the road when this part of Albert Gate was demolished.* PLYMOUTH NAVAL BASE MUSEUM

These two late 1960s views of the North Yard loco shed show its stone-built rear and corrugated iron front section.
D KIVER COLLECTION

To construct the Keyham Steam Yard a considerable retaining wall was necessary, leaving a narrow defile to the rear of the Quadrangle building, known ever since as the 'Narrows' Through this squeezed both the railway and the road, here seen looking north on 31 March 1977.
COLLECTION P. BURKHALTER

TOP RIGHT: *Seen from the opposite end, the Narrows was bridged to allow access by pedestrians to Keyham College, located above the wall on the left. Rail tracks radiate out in the foreground. March 1977.*
COLLECTION P. BURKHALTER

Looking south towards the Narrows, where a southbound passenger train is in the loop waiting to depart. PLYMOUTH NAVAL BASE MUSEUM

CONNECTION TO THE CORNWALL RAILWAY

The southern approaches to the exchange sidings were relaid c1954, here a temporary diversion takes No. 2 on a southbound freight around new trackage outside the Torpedo Shop. PLYMOUTH NAVAL BASE MUSEUM

BOTTOM LEFT: *Post-war improvements included the complete relaying of the area adjacent to St Levans Gate, to the south of the sidings. Here a crossover into the Works Department Yard is being put in c1954. On the left of the three workmen is Bernard Taylor, who spent almost all his working life looking after the permanent way in the Dockyard.* PLYMOUTH NAVAL BASE MUSEUM

The centre disc of one of the two turntables located outside the Torpedo Shop in North Yard, with all vital information cast thereon. 1992. In late 1995 it was purchased by the Shakerstone Railway, and moved to Leicestershire. P. BURKHALTER

35

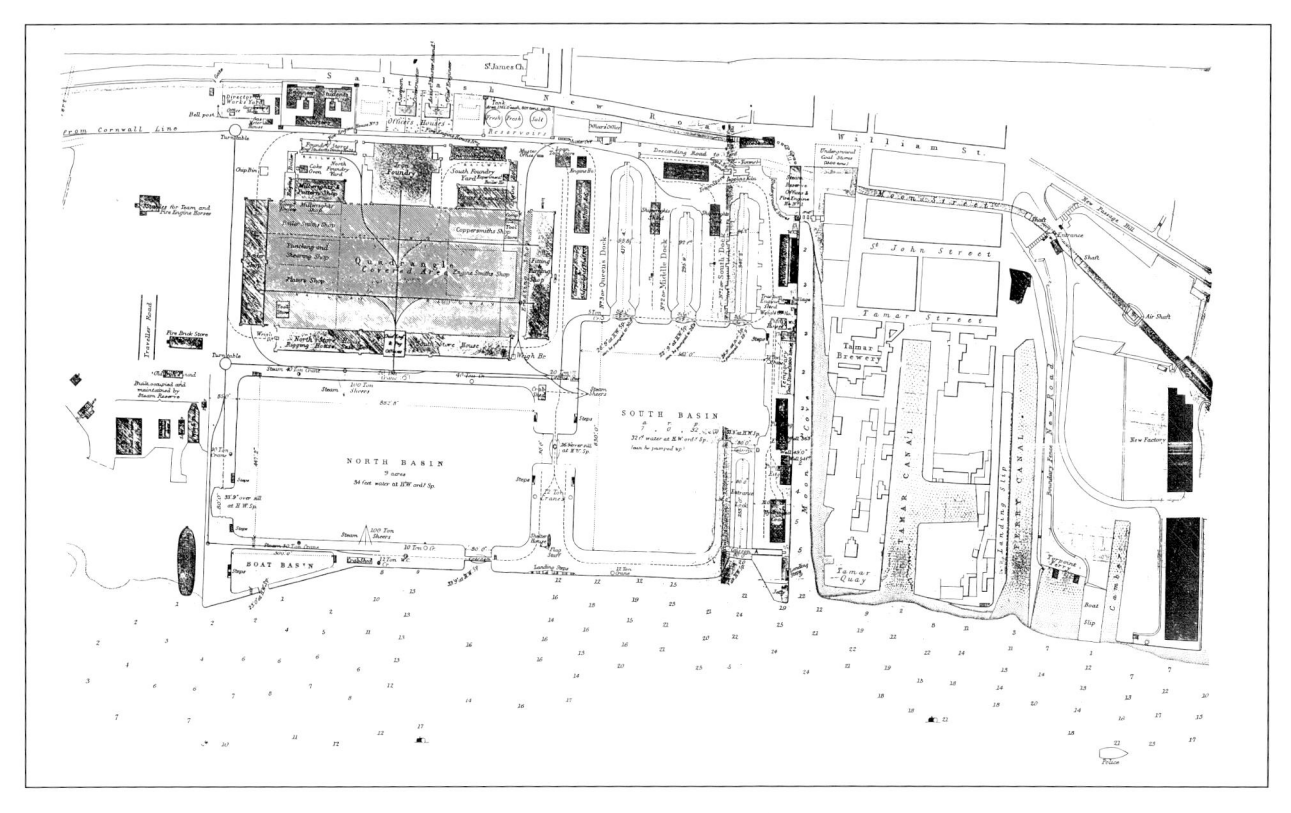

1879 Yard Plan

The Admiralty allowed the Cornwall Railway to stable on the branch the spare rolling stock which had brought exhibits for a visit of the Bath & West of England Show in 1872, staged on the fields where Central Park is now located.

Having only ten years prior constructed the railway from Keyham into Devonport Yard, dissatisfaction at the constraints on traffic arising from the restricted size of the tunnel between the two Yards was becoming apparent. On Saturday 27 February 1886 a delegation from the Great Western Railway, including Mr Margary the Engineer, visited the Yard. The purpose was to examine ways of improving the connection from the main-line to Devonport Yard, particularly for passenger carriages to reach a proposed jetty for embarkation of seamen and troops. Not surprisingly 'it is anticipated that some alterations will be necessary in a tunnel'. Nothing came out of this initiative and the operating difficulties continued.

The remoteness of Keyham Junction was ended with the construction of the Royal Naval Barracks, now known as HMS Drake, situated on the land between the branch railway and the mud flats of the Hamoaze north of the Keyham Steam Yard. Construction was completed so that the first sailors could occupy them in June 1889, and the main entrance to the Barracks was located on a new bridge built over the branch. A report dated 5 December 1883 dealt with many aspects of the design of the layout of the new facilities, *inter-alia* it recommended two platforms with separate shelters for officers and for men should be provided on either side of the railway near the Guard House. Steps from railway to ground level should be inside the main gates under the observation of the Guard. In 1886 brief consideration was given to doubling the branch at an estimated cost of £3,000. But the level of traffic was not considered sufficient to justify this move, however it concluded with an intriguing statement; 'it does not appear there should be much difficulty.... in working shuttle trains. No doubt more rolling stock will be required in the shape of 3rd class carriages'. Was this a reference to an imminent commencement of an early passenger service in the Dockyard?

The original plans provided for a platform of some 50 yards in length on both sides of the single line track with staircases rising to the road level above. In the event only one platform was ever built, completed in 1886 at a cost of £500. This was located on the west side of the track whereas the standard gauge rails were offset to the east, but quite how the gap was bridged between standard gauge trains and the platform edge is not recorded. The permanent platform was increased in length at the outset of the First War in 1914 to 90 yards by a timber boarded extension to the north, in the cutting approach to the Junction. This resulted in a very narrow width of platform through the bridge and to ease the exit of passengers an additional staircase was provided to the north of the bridge, with a gate through the Barracks fence at the top. At this time the plans also indicate that the original permanent platform had a roof. At the time of writing (1995) the stonework of the bridge adjacent to the platform bears the outline of a roof which could have been that over the platform. The timber platform extension was eventually removed as it had become rotten, but not until the 1970s.

One other facility for the Barracks also completed mid-1886 was a coal Storage Pound, holding 600 tons, served by a siding leading off the branch, at a cost of £600. This survived until after the Second World War, and the long sleepers for the turnout were not finally removed until 1992.

The broad gauge met its final demise over the weekend of 20-22 May 1892. Much has been written on the massive task that the Great Western undertook, which need not concern us here. Every detail was meticulously planned and included ensuring that all wagons on private branches, such as that to the Dockyard, were removed in early May. Whilst the conversion of the main line was fully executed over that eventful weekend it seems the private branches were left behind. A photograph taken in 1896, some 4 years after the conversion, clearly shows the third rail still in place at the site of the Exchange Sidings. It is probable that this was only

c1883 Seaman's Barracks entrance proposal showing the planned (but never built) double platform arrangement.

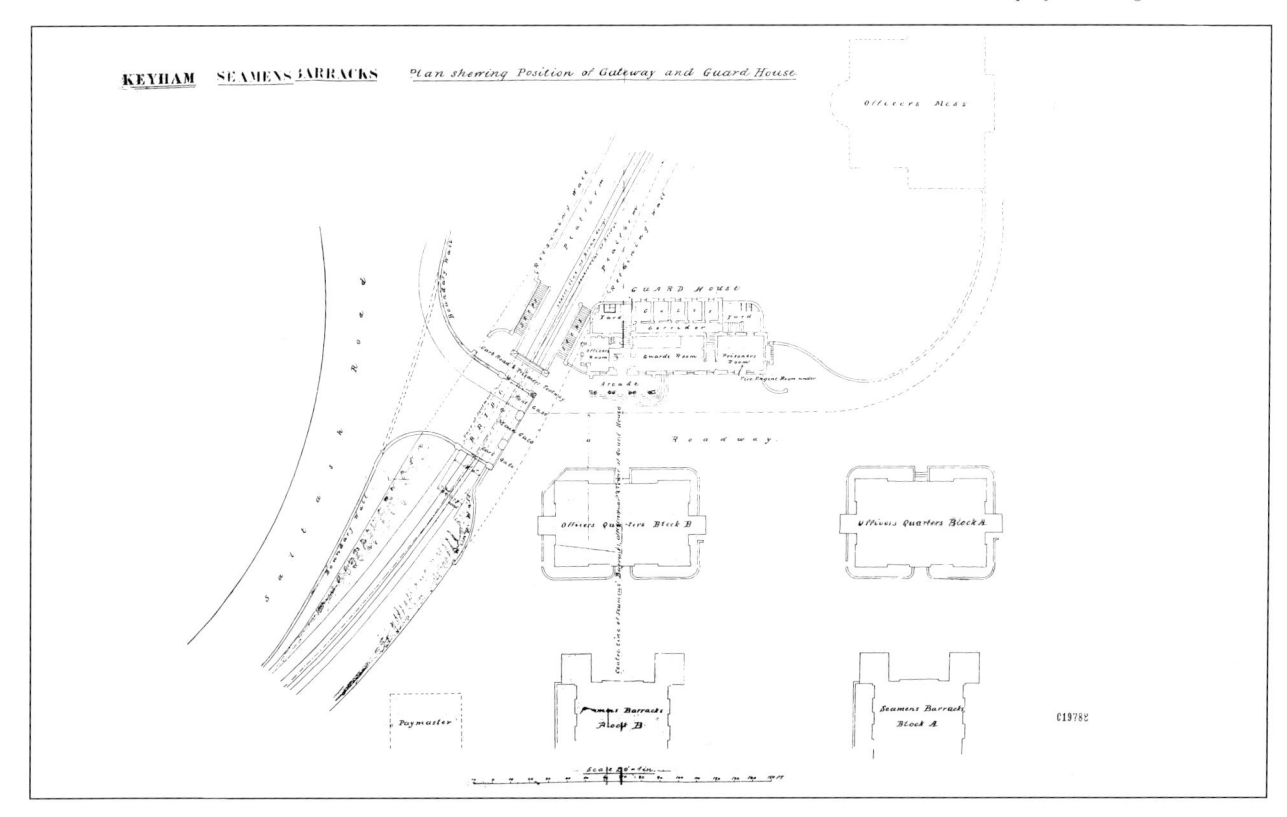

c1889, and the last few years' use of the mixed gauge on the branch. The Commodore's House in the Barracks grounds was built sandwiched between the railway and the public road (Saltash Road). The Main Gate bridge is seen at the left.
PUBLIC RECORD OFFICE ADM195/60

This early (c1889) view of the Barracks shows the railway left. This picture epitomises the remoteness of the locality when the Navy built the establishment. In the background are the fields of Barne Barton, now completely filled with housing.
COLLECTION P. BURKHALTER

CONNECTION TO THE CORNWALL RAILWAY

ABOVE: In this postcard view of the Barracks, possibly just after the First War, can be glimpsed a closed van on the coal yard siding.
COLLECTION P. BURKHALTER

That the railway is unfenced in the grounds of HMS Drake can be clearly seen. The road crossing is to a car park. February 1992. DEVONPORT MANAGEMENT LTD.

TOP LEFT: No record has come to light that dates the last use of the Admiralty Platform. It is now occupied by a concrete garage, though the platform edge white line is maintained. 24 February 1995.
P. BURKHALTER

North British built type 2 diesel-hydraulic D6309 slowly passes through the leafy surroundings of HMS Drake in June 1967 with an inbound freight.
CHRIS HORSHAM

39

A view looking towards the rail gate to HMS Drake from Keyham Junction. The far track is the headshunt lifted just after this photograph was taken in February 1992. The wooden building is 'Camels Head Signal Box'. The author sports fine headwear.
DEVONPORT MANAGEMENT LTD.

Keyham West Ground Frame in February 1992. The following year a steel floor with metal handrails replaced the timber arrangements seen here.
DEVONPORT MANAGEMENT LTD.

In February 1992 the branch had not seen any traffic for some time, as the rusty rails indicate. In the vee of the tracks is Keyham West Ground Frame, with the mainline westwards over Weston Mill Viaduct in the distance. DEVONPORT MANAGEMENT LTD.

removed when new sidings were installed in 1904.

During the annual inspections of the Plymouth Naval facilities by the Lords of the Admiralty, which usually occupied two days each summer during the 1880s and 1890s, it was the regular practice to transport the visitors between the Yards and the Barracks in a special railway saloon.

The original timber structure of Weston Mill Viaduct lasted until 1899 when a contract was let to J. Charles Lang of Liskeard for the replacement. If the timber construction could be considered flimsy, then the opposite was true of its successor. This was the massive brick and steel crossing that exists to this day.

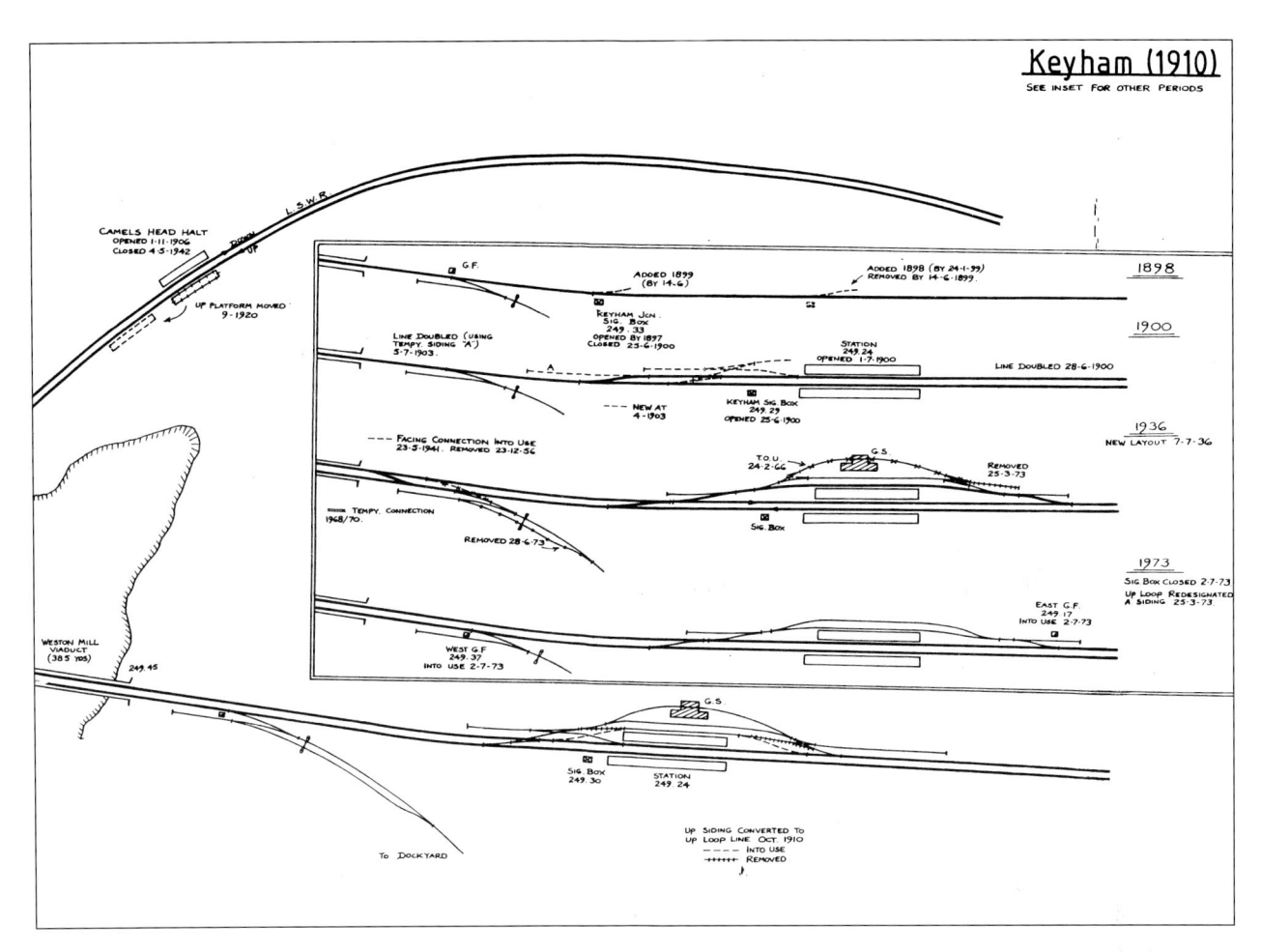

Developments at Keyham
R.A. COOKE

From the headshunt in February 1992. Under the road bridge is Keyham Station. DEVONPORT MANAGEMENT LTD.

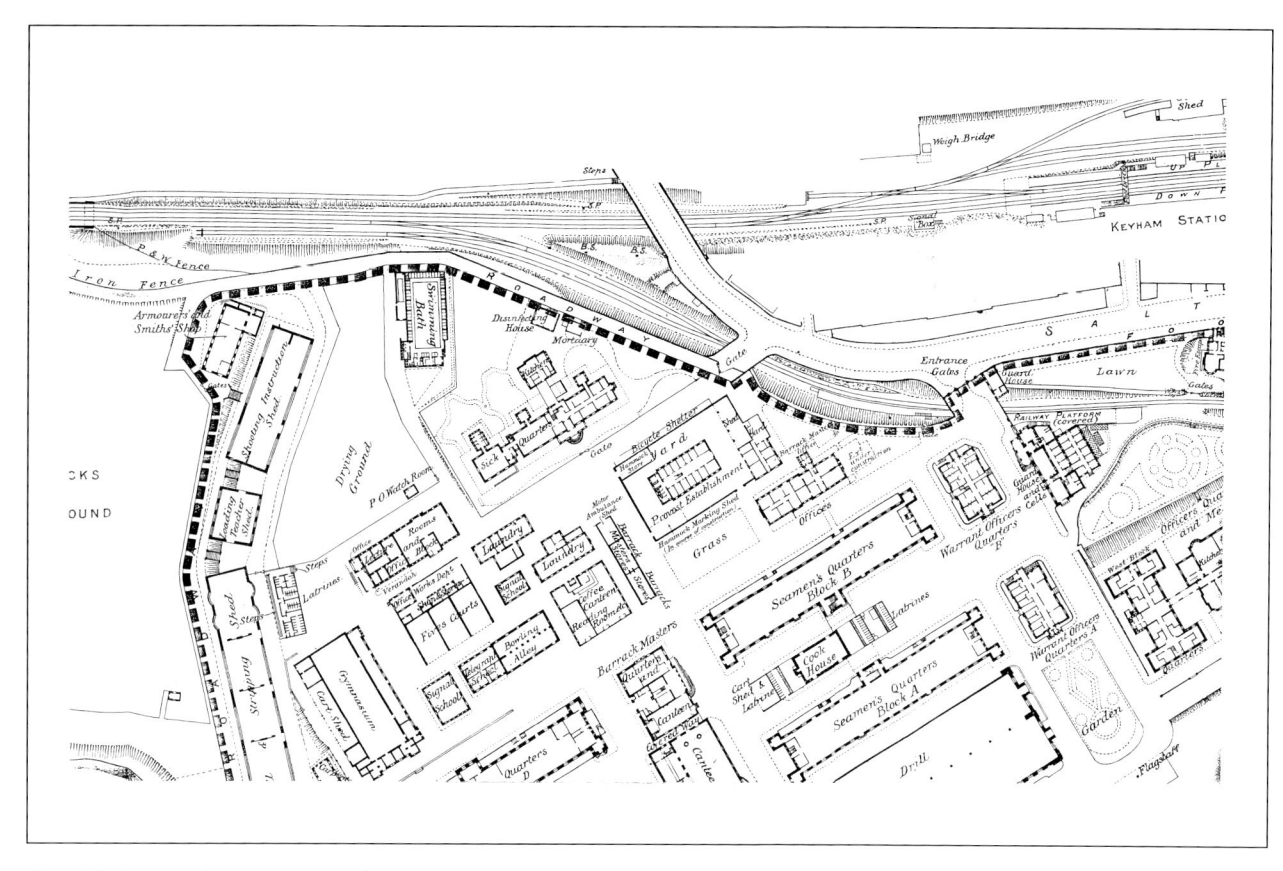

Plan of Keyham Junction

Keyham GWR station, probably in the 1920s. Beyond the overbridge in the distance is the junction with the Dockyard branch.
COLLECTION P. BURKHALTER

Sited to the west of the old viaduct, and raised up by the 15 feet mentioned above to ease the dip in the line, it was completed in 1903. The gradients either side of Weston Mill were eased out to 1 in 200 and 1 in 400 respectively on the approach embankments and brick spans This resulted in some height being added to the level at Keyham Junction, changing the level section at the northern end of the branch to a 1 in 91 gradient. It is obvious that alterations were necessary to the branch trackwork to connect to the new line. The opportunity was taken to straighten out the main line, which meandered slightly where Keyham Station is now. To allow for the new viaduct, the cutting walls were cut back and the branch slewed over towards the west, as the original trackbed of the headshunt siding was needed for the approaches to the new viaduct.

The opening of the Barracks could not be ignored by the Great Western Railway, and at the same time as the Weston Mill Viaduct was re-constructed, and the approach lines realigned, the opportunity was taken to construct a brand new station, called Keyham. This was also to serve the considerable housing development in the area, which had grown up to serve the new Naval installations. The station opened on 1 July 1900, just three days after the doubling of the former single track line westward from Plymouth. Initially it was a plain two platform affair, but a goods

CONNECTION TO THE CORNWALL RAILWAY

Keyham Station in May 1922. This view is taken from the approach road to the goods yard, and the wagons seen were possibly from the Dockyard, awaiting collection.
COLLECTION P. BURKHALTER

yard was in place by April 1903. The main line doubling could be continued westward across the new Weston Mill Viaduct once that was completed on 3 July 1903. The siding to the rear of the up platform at Keyham was converted into a full loop with connections at both ends and the platform was widened at the same time, all being brought into use in February 1911.

The junction between the Dockyard Railway and the mainline was a westward facing connection. We have seen earlier that a headshunt siding was installed in 1867, and at some stage after this a short loop no longer than 50 yards appears between the junction and the northern access bridge to the Barracks. At the time of the viaduct reconstruction and other works the loop was extended to lead into the headshunt. This work was done in connection with the doubling by the GWR.

To ensure the security of the Barracks massive timber gates were installed conveniently sited under the northernmost bridge over the branch, completely closing the arch. This arrangement lasted until recent years when a wire mesh gate replaced the wooden doors.

We have seen above that the L&SWR gained access to Plymouth via the Great Western's Launceston branch. Soon the South Western sought authority for its own line into the town, down the Tamar valley. This was the Plymouth, Devonport & South Western Junction Railway, which opened from Lydford on 2 June 1890. The approach to Plymouth ran parallel to the Great Western from the Royal Albert Bridge towards Devonport, and passengers from the new housing developments were amply catered for with new stations and halts.

A Southern freight arrives in Keyham Station with a transfer for the Dockyard, with class O2 30225 based at Friary shed in charge. LARRY CROSIER

43

Class 25 (25171) shunts a Dockyard bound freight in the back road of Keyham Station on 18 April 1975. C Horsham

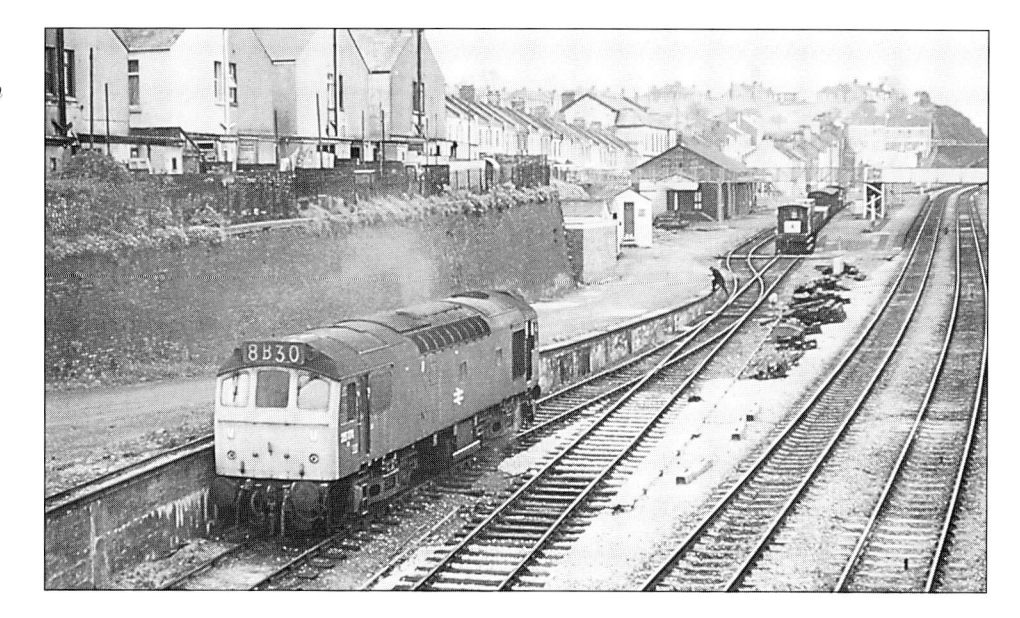

This superb aerial view taken c1988, shows Keyham Station, with Keyham Junction on the right. The branch runs in a cutting, then away to top right and the exchange sidings. Devonport Management Ltd.

CHAPTER FIVE

LATE NINETEENTH CENTURY EXTENSIONS TO THE DOCKYARD

As the nineteenth century progressed into its second half so expectations rose for more expansion to the size of the Dockyard. Whilst the new docks and facilities forming Keyham Steam Yard were adequate when built, technology was moving on, and ships were being built larger and larger in size.

So the Dockyard required enhanced facilities. To this end a survey of the area to the north of the (then new) Steam Yard was undertaken in December 1859. Nothing came of this, nor did any progress result from a 1890 plan of expansion; this latter scheme proposed to use 1,500 convicts in construction gangs.

Finally the Naval Works Act of 1895 provided for a vast undertaking which would double the size of all the existing facilities of Keyham and Devonport Yards together. This was to occupy 118 acres, of which only 41 acres were above the high water mark. The works were huge; two wet basins (one tidal and one closed, respectively 10 and 35 ½ acres),

1888 Yard Plan

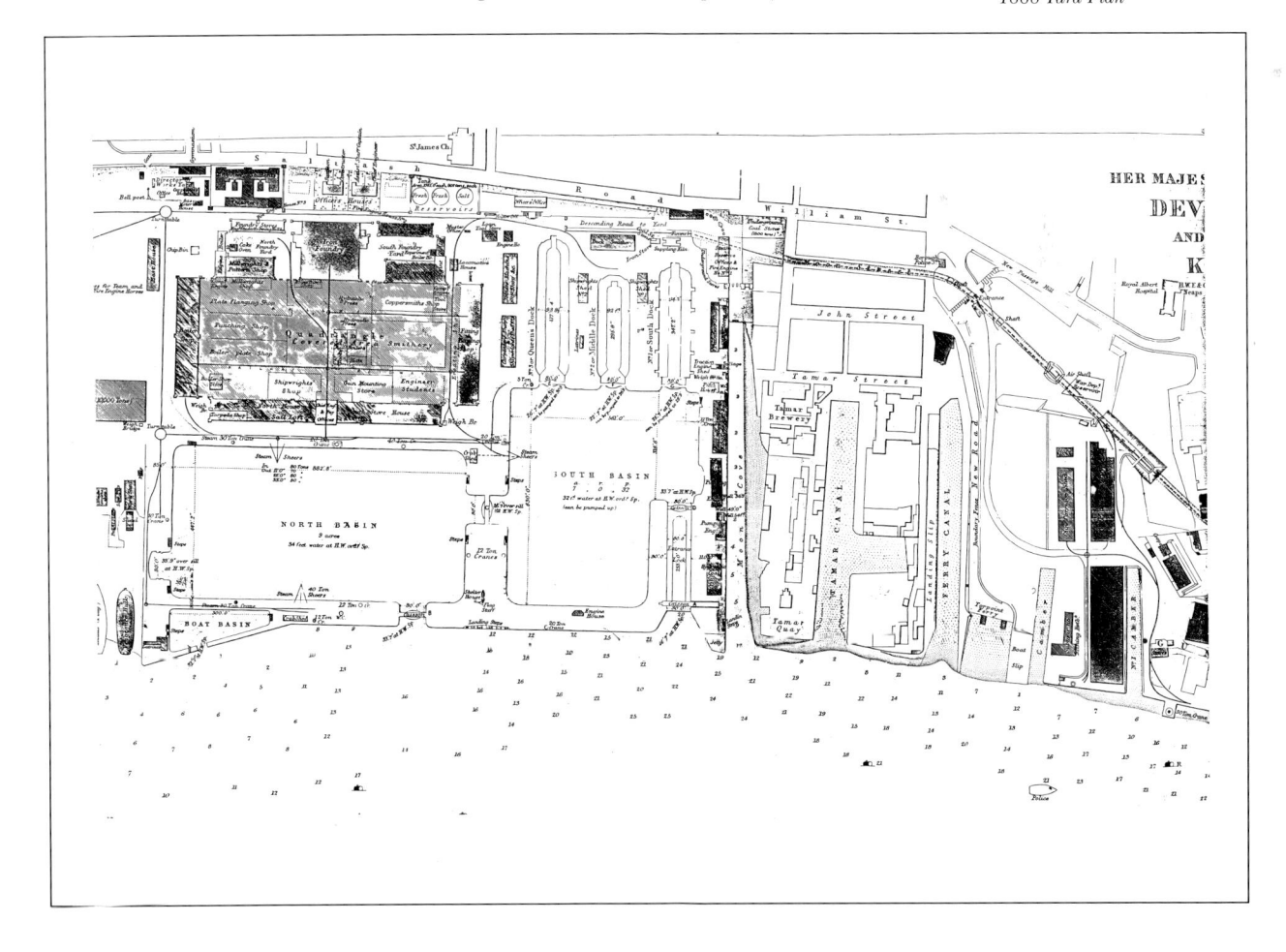

45

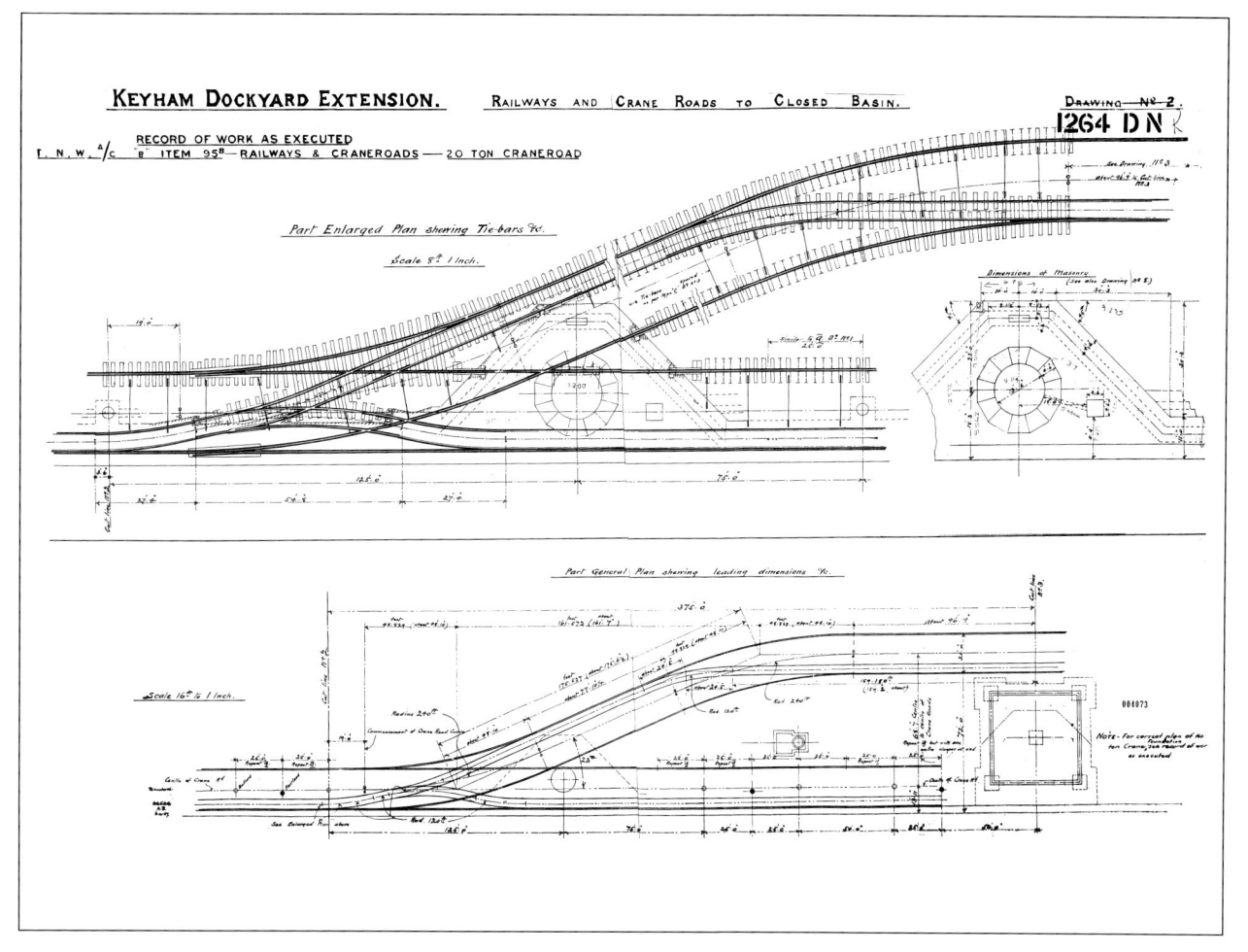

c1899 Extension Works plans of railways at the Cantilever Crane, on the eastern wall of the Closed Basin.

an entrance lock 730 feet long to the closed basin, plus a tidal entrance and three dry docks 120 feet wide and 480, 711 and 715 feet long. The site was partly tidal mud flat and foreshore. For the exclusion of water from the work area a cofferdam 7,600 feet long was constructed, costructed of pine piles up to 75 feet long and specially obtained from America. The full story of this eleven year job would be inappropriate here but some of the constructional details will lend an appropriate background.

Six contractors submitted prices in September 1895 in answer to the Admiralty's specifications and Bill of Quantities dated July 1895. Although the tender was accepted on 1 January 1896, a lengthy period ensued before an agreement, with amendments, with Sir John Jackson, Contractors, of Victoria Street, Westminster, London was signed on 13 October 1896, at a price of £2,932,571.2s.4d.

John Jackson was born in York in 1851, and was knighted in 1895 for his work in completing the Manchester Ship Canal after the first contractor failed. A man who involved himself in great construction works, he offered at one point to build the British half of a bridge across the English Channel. Whilst the Keyham undertaking was in progress he lived at Pounds House, in what is now Central Park, and was elected Unionist MP for Devonport from 1910 until he retired from Parliament in 1918. He died on 14 December 1919 whilst visiting friends in Godalming. The company became Sir John Jackson Limited in 1898.

Relevant to this book are the temporary railways used in connection with the construction, and the permanent tracks and other related work in the finished job.

JACKSON'S TEMPORARY RAILWAYS

No plans have survived of any of these lines, but fortunately over 300 record photographs give us a vivid picture of all the aspects of the construction. From these we can piece together the layout of Jackson's temporary tracks, which did service for 11 years. A contemporary press report stated that 25 miles of such railways were employed and that as early as July 1896 eleven locomotives were on the works.

Most of the site was covered in deep mud. The original intention had been for this to be excavated by steam navvies (excavator cranes), tipped into rail wagons and hauled to tipping stages on the river to be taken away in barges. It transpired that the mud was too soft to support this equipment, and a change of plan was needed. This resulted in an arrangement whereby a large metal scoop was hauled across the area by a wire suspended from the top of high towers, to be tipped directly into barges. This method turned out to be somewhat impractical as the scoops tended to follow the first channel they had cut, so once the rock or other firmer ground had been exposed the conventional excavator and rail haulage was resorted to, working from the base of this trench. The temporary rail tracks led to the foot of inclines (one was at the south-east corner of the closed basin) where the filled wagons were hauled up utilising the steam engines that had earlier operated the scoops. At ground level the wagons were then hauled round to the water's edge for tipping into barges, or the mud was used as general fill.

At the very start of the massive Extension works contract, on 17 April 1896, Jackson's railway stock is working to fill Keyham Lake. In the background the houses in Saltash Road stand behind the Yard wall, before which is the single track branch from the GWR. On the extreme right is a glimpse of the original timber St Levans Viaduct on the mainline. PUBLIC RECORD OFFICE ADM195/61

One of Jackson's loco's stands at the foot of an access incline, leading down to the excavations for the docks. 11 May 1900
PUBLIC RECORD OFFICE
ADM195/61

The cableways left some areas untouched close to the sides in the corners of the closed basin. Here the mud was still too soft for conventional standard gauge locomotives and wagons. Therefore 2 feet 6 inch gauge, one cubic yard, side tip wagons, built on site, with 15 inch wheels, were filled by hand and hauled up inclines by winding engines to tip into conventional wagons for dispatch to the dump stage. Narrow gauge tramways were also used in the tidal basin area.

Some of the excavated waste material from the site was taken by trains of wagons to an area north of the Barracks, west of Weston Mill Viaduct, to infill part of Weston Mill Lake. At the completion of this operation it was covered in topsoil and grassed as a new recreation ground for the Barracks, a function it still performs today. The rock that was excavated was needed for backfilling behind the finished dock walls, so this was stockpiled in the area of the closed basin.

Huge quantities of shingle were dredged from the sea, firstly off Start Bay, south Devon, and later from off the Needles on the Isle of Wight. All this material was brought in by sea to a rail served landing stage constructed into the river at the south end of the works. On the staging were four 10 ton steam cranes which worked 24 hours a day landing about 35,000 tons per month. The approach was by a double track railway on staging, leading to two parallel platforms with run-around tracks interlaced with the 7 feet gauge crane tracks. The goods landed included 2,200 tons per month of cement in sacks, which was hauled to the cement sheds, and 2,500 tons of granite each month which went to the stacking yards. The total volume of granite was a staggering 2,342,000 cubic feet. By far the largest volumes were the vast quantities of shingle, at the rate of 25,000 tons per month. Other requirements delivered by sea and hauled by rail were limestone, broken stone, timber and coal.

All the concrete (1,230,500 cubic yards of it) was mixed in six centrally placed gas powered concrete mixers placed under two stages to which double track rail inclines ran so that the aggregate and cement could be supplied from above. Once mixed the wet concrete could be discharged into wagons for delivery to the place of working. Where this was in the bottom of the docks then the concrete skip wagons were lowered down rope worked inclines to be loco hauled to where needed.

The large amount of plant and equipment on the site required extensive workshop facilities and a smithy, fitting shop and carpenters shops were located in the south-east corner of the site, adjacent to where the new pumping station was to stand. All kinds of boiler repairs were undertaken, with mixed success, and even complete rebuilds were carried out. One end of the fitting shop provided for a locomotive shed accommodating 18 engines.

A rail connection to the Dockyard system, and therefore via that to the GWR, was established at a very early date, soon after March 1896. This allowed for direct rail deliveries into the site, and was situated at the foot of the gradient from Keyham, just

This fine view of the construction of the entrance lock to the closed basin, clearly shows the extensive temporary works required for such an undertaking. On 18 July 1903 the locomotive CLYDE (Manning Wardle 714) poses with crew for the photographer.
PUBLIC RECORD OFFICE
ADM195/61

No. 121 EXCAVATION IN CLOSED BASIN FEBY 1905.

In the middle of the excavation of the closed basin a locomotive service point, with water tank and coaling stage. In February 1905 one of the Barclay locomotives stands while another 'speeds' past. PUBLIC RECORD OFFICE ADM195/61

Sir John Jackson's railway required many and varied wagons. Here a 4 wheel block flat bed, number 294, has just been unloaded. PUBLIC RECORD OFFICE ADM195/61

outside the then Keyham Yard north wall. However conflicts over the use of the existing Admiralty lines is evident in a report in August 1897; 'the dockyard train runs.... when the track is not monopolised by the tyrannical contractor'.

A report in July 1899 listed the mechanical plant and included the fourteen locomotives in use at that time. Four were six-wheeled, with 15-inch cylinders and the rest were four-wheeled. They were from Barclay, Manning Wardle, Hunslet Engine Co., Hudswell Clarke, and Hawthorn Leslie and Co. A total of 25 engines were eventually used here and full details are listed elsewhere.

Other railway equipment was an extensive fleet of side tip four-wheel wagons, plus a variety of flat trucks for carrying dressed stone and other non-granular goods. Some closed stores vans were also seen. At the closing auction most of this rolling stock was put on the market, and whilst most of it were items one would have expected to see, there were included two passenger coaches. Quite what function these performed has not been recorded but it can be imagined that the senior officials on the site could have been transported around to inspect the works in rail borne carriages and so avoid the clinging mud.

The one principal mishap concerning the Contractor's railway during this vast undertaking, with tragic consequences, was the boiler explosion to Manning Wardle No 951 *Accrington* (subsequently re-named *Devonport*) on Monday 3 November 1902. The crew consisted of driver Fred Long, fireman John Barretto, and rope runner (shunter) George Comstack, all of whom had been working on the loco that morning since 6 a.m. At 11.30 they had worked out to the jetty and picked up eight trucks of ballast, each about 5 tons. On the run to the yard, when near the new pumping station, a tube burst at the front of the boiler enveloping the engine in steam. This in itself was not too much of a problem but in jumping off the locomotive the nineteen year old fireman Barretto became entangled in the following wagons and was killed. The inquest on the following Wednesday conducted by the local coroner Mr J. A. Pearce recorded a verdict of accidental death. The Board of Trade boiler inspector conducted an inquiry and found that a wasting of one of the top tubes at the front end had caused it to collapse. This was despite the engine having been almost totally rebuilt at Keyham in October 1900 (a plate being attached to the engine to that effect). The inspector reported that new tubes had been ordered, but the examination before the accident had not been accompanied by a hydraulic test. Had it done so the loco may have been stopped and the accident averted.

Other mishaps occurred, for on 1 September 1899 a Mr J Winter, an Inspector of the works, was knocked down by a truck being propelled by a locomotive, and suffered a broken hip. Then on Thursday 6 February 1902 a twenty-eight year old labourer by the name of Charles Peacock was run over by the locomotive *Mount Edgecumbe* (Manning Wardle No 1342) and killed. The crew of the locomotive, driver Frederick Perry and rope runner John Colley, had no opportunity of halting the train, which consisted of five wagons.

Just to the north of Keyham Junction is Weston Mill Viaduct. This view taken in December 1896 principally to show the coffer dam construction, also shows the original Brunel timber viaduct, one of many on the Cornwall Railway, and nicely captures the rather rickety nature of its construction. PUBLIC RECORD OFFICE ADM195/61

This superb panoramic view of the Extension works in c1902 has at least six of Jackson's locomotives in sight.
COLLECTION P. BURKHALTER

The long project is nearly complete in December 1906, here No.8 dock is on the left, with a collection of the contractors rolling stock in the centre. On the extreme right is the branch railway from Keyham Junction emerging from the Barracks through a gateway, still standing today.
PUBLIC RECORD OFFICE
ADM195/61

LATE 19TH CENTURY EXTENSIONS TO THE YARD

Though the print is a little damaged, this is a unique view of Sir John Jackson's yard, just at the end of his contract in December 1906. Much can be seen, especially the L&SWR wagon, having been transferred from the branch on the site railway via a connection off to the bottom left, also various boilers lying around, and in the background the newly built dock pumping station. PUBLIC RECORD OFFICE ADM195/61

53

This fine view of the Exchange Sidings in its original form was taken on 21 September 1971, immediately before the alterations for the New Combined Pipeshop. To the left of the flagman's cabin is the abandoned track of the mainline northwards. The later route north was on the track in the left foreground.
COLLECTION P. BURKHALTER

PERMANENT RAILS IN THE EXTENSION

From the outset the Dockyard's own railway system was to be extended into the new works on completion. 4,700 yards of track were to be laid, of which 1,000 yards were curved. There were to be nine sets of ordinary turnouts, and one diamond crossing. The specification called for flat bottom rails of 75lb per yard weight fixed to the sleepers with wood screws and clips to standard gauge. Crossings and switches were to be held in chairs and constructed of the same weight rail. In all the total cost of these items was tendered at £9,240.12s.6d.

Although the plans show turntables in the Extension Yard area, none appear in Jackson's contract. It would seem that the Admiralty decided to purchase these themselves.

The construction of the Extension Works required the removal of a long landing stage projecting 1,200 feet westwards into the Hamoaze which permitted river access to the Barracks. This had been built as recently as 1890 and therefore only lasted some six years. There was some form of tramway on its considerable length. Replacement facilities by way of a stone wharf were built at the northwest corner of the Barracks grounds on Weston Mill Lake, and to connect with this a light narrow gauge railway was installed which ran to the stores yard at the south end of the Barracks. A branch turned off next to the Parade Ground along to the church. It is evident from contemporary plans that this was not a locomotive worked system as no run round loops were provided. It can be assumed that as abundant man-power would have been available such luxury would not have been required. After 1914 however the railway had disappeared from the plans so it appears that this was a short lived arrangement.

One of the jobs undertaken by Jackson was for a fan of reception sidings on the Branch. This was located on the alignment of the incoming line, between the South Barrack Gate and the Dockyard lines. Three parallel roads were installed between September 1903 and June 1904, and these would have greatly helped by providing a reception facility instead of having trains running directly onto the Dockyard tracks inside St Levans Gate. However this location was on the 1 in 70 gradient from Keyham close to its foot and from time to time caused problems, as we shall read later.

Finally the works were completed, some three years later than envisaged, on 31 December 1906, and at a final cost of over £4,000,000. The first ship to enter the Tidal Basin was the *HMS Royal Sovereign* in early August 1906, then on the tenth of that month *HMS Hibernia* was docked down in No 9 Dock via the Tidal Basin. On 21 February 1907 their Royal Highnesses the Prince and Princess of Wales sailed into the closed basin via the lock to officially open the entire scheme.

Over 3,500 men had been employed in the works, and it can be imagined that the opening was accompanied with much pomp. The arrangements for conveying the royal party to the site were by river, it being deemed impractical to drive through the streets of Devonport. This apparent affront to the town resulted in the event being boycotted by the Mayor and Burgesses of the town. Sir John Jackson hosted a large party of seventy of his own guests, for which he chartered a special train from Paddington to Millbay, arriving at 8.55 p.m. the previous evening. It comprised six coaches, including first class dining cars, and returned to London on the day of the opening at 6 p.m.

At the completion of the contract a large auction was held, by the firm of Wheatley, Kirk, Price & Co. of 46 Watling Street, London, over the period of a week, commencing on 30 January 1907. 1,370 lots were put on sale, of which those relating to the railway equipment were:

18 locomotives (earlier advertisements stated 19)
246 ballast wagons
189 side-tip wagons
24 end-tip wagons
13 bolster wagons
17 flat top wagons
11 covered cement wagons
36 concrete bogies
2 passenger coaches
500 tons steel rail (later changed to 1500 tons)

Details of the locomotives sold are recorded later but some strangers were mentioned in the press reports of the auction, such as *Lord Kitchener* £210 and *Saltash* (4 wheel) £235. Quite which of the locomotives these were is not now known, perhaps they were included in the sale for convenience, but located elsewhere. Something to confirm this theory is that the engine *Methil* (4 wheel coupled saddle tank, sold for £80) is mentioned, and this is believed to be Andrew Barclay works number 178 that was at a contract of Jackson's on the Firth of Forth concurrently with the Keyham works.

During the alterations of the Exchange Sidings in 1972, they were moved some twenty feet to the east, and set into a concrete apron flush with the rails. Here a mixed freight awaits attention, whilst a load of plate has been turned ready for the passage of the tunnel to South Yard.
COLLECTION P. BURKHALTER

The site of the future Exchange Sidings photographed on 28 April 1896, looking 'uphill'. The most significant feature is the third, broad gauge, rail, still in place some four years after its removal from the mainline.
PUBLIC RECORD OFFICE
ADM195/61

At almost exactly the same location 96 years later with great changes to be seen, except that the row of houses with the bay window in the end is still in view (though since demolished).
DEVONPORT MANAGEMENT LTD.

CHAPTER SIX

INTO THE TWENTIETH CENTURY

In Devonport Yard a new slipway, later to be known as No 3 slip, for the building of Naval ships was commenced in mid-1900, a Plymouth contractor G. Shellabear & Son being awarded the £60,000 contract. Included in the contract were new railways to connect with the existing lines in the area.

In conjunction with the Extension Works were built many ancillary buildings. One was the large Torpedo Shop, just to the north of St Levans Gate. To provide for the movement of the torpedoes a 2 feet 6 inch gauge tram track inset into the cobbles was laid to the rear of the building to move them into the separate Test House. It is assumed that the trolleys were pushed by hand.

In the early days of January 1905 the next locomotive arrived for the Dockyard, and this was a most unusual type. Supplied by Hawthorn Leslie of Newcastle it was a 4 ton crane engine. Pivoted in the centre of the boiler was a crane jib powered though gearing from a separate set of steam cylinders. What is not known is which Yard this engine operated in, as it obviously could not pass through the tunnel, although sometime in the 1930s it was converted into a conventional locomotive, in the Dockyard's own workshops, it is said.

TUNNEL ACCIDENT

The third documented railway fatality occurred on Saturday, 6 July 1907. At 8.10 a.m. a Post Office telegraph boy, Arthur Mitchell, aged 15 and stationed at Devonport Post Office, was given a message to deliver to North Yard. For reasons that were never established he decided to pass through South Yard and jump on a train to get to North Yard, despite an instruction to travel directly there on the public highway.

At this time the single line through the tunnel was controlled by bell signals operated by signalmen in small 'boxes' at either end. On the morning in question, the South signalman, one William Moon of Saltash, rang the code needed to ask the North signalman, to allow a special through. The special was a single flat truck belonging to the Great Western Railway hauled by No 5. Having apparently received the all-clear, he gave the driver a shout to go ahead, this being the method at the time. As he did so the messenger boy jumped on the flat truck and sat facing rearwards swinging his legs off the end. Although the passenger service had been running for some time it was common practice for people to jump on freight trains, although this was not permitted. The signalman said nothing, not that anything could be done about stopping the train receding into the tunnel.

But there had been a dramatic misunderstanding in the sending and receiving of the bell signals, as the 'question' on the bells 'Is the line clear?' was the same as the answer 'The line is clear'. What appeared to have happened was that the lack of difference in these signals resulted in trains being dispatched simultaneously from both ends of the tunnel. For after the 8.15 a.m. southbound passenger had left the North Yard, a freight came up comprising *Middlesbrough* and seven trucks, six of which were loaded with armour plating steel plate for the *HMS Temeraire* which was being built on No 3 building slip (at the time the largest ship to have been built in Devonport). This train was given the all clear at the same time as No 5, as both signalmen had understood that they each had received the 'all-clear'.

57

The southbound train moved off slowly, for not only was it heavily loaded but a horse drawn cart was preceding it down the ramp to get to the Coal Yard. The lightly loaded northbound train therefore had got much further in the tunnel and had passed around the sharp bend when it came upon *Middlesbrough*. The driver of the southbound train was fortunately keeping a good eye open and had the shock of seeing the approaching engine appear round the bend. He had the presence of mind to shut off steam, applied the brake, and reversed, but all this did was to reduce the speed to 3 or 4 miles per hour. The two trains collided, and the much heavier southbound locomotive and train forced No 5 about 100 yards back down the line and up onto the flat truck with its chimney jammed into the tunnel roof.

Young Arthur Mitchell suffered fatal injuries and died on his way to hospital. The driver and fireman of No 5 also had been injured sufficiently to require hospital treatment, but *Middlesbrough's* crew were attended to in the Dockyard surgery.

Both No 5 and the truck it was pulling seem to have been sufficiently damaged to justify scrapping. The locomotive's chimney was broken off, both ends of the engine severely smashed, and it came to rest at an angle of 45 degrees. On the other hand *Middlesbrough* could be driven back to the North Yard shed after another engine had pulled away the loaded trucks. It was the following day before rail services could resume.

An inquest was held the following Monday in the Guildhall. Fairly intense questioning produced the evidence that the system had the inherent defect of potential misunderstanding; the bells not being sufficiently clear as to whether they were asking or receiving the 'all-clear'. The Coroner seemed to have been adequately versed in the art of railway signalling and control to be able to ask whether there should be a block staff system. This point totally disconcerted the Dockyard authorities, who did not know what he was talking about. They quickly became knowledgeable enough to order a Miniature Staff installation, which is dealt with in the signalling chapter. The verdict of the Coroner's jury was that the system of signalling trains through was defective so that neither signalman could be held entirely to blame. They made the recommendation that the Dockyard authorities should adopt an improved method of signals. A telling closing statement by the father of the dead boy, told of times when he saw every truck, open and closed, packed 'like sardines' and that a more terrible accident could happen.

Plan of 5 Basin showing World War One platforms

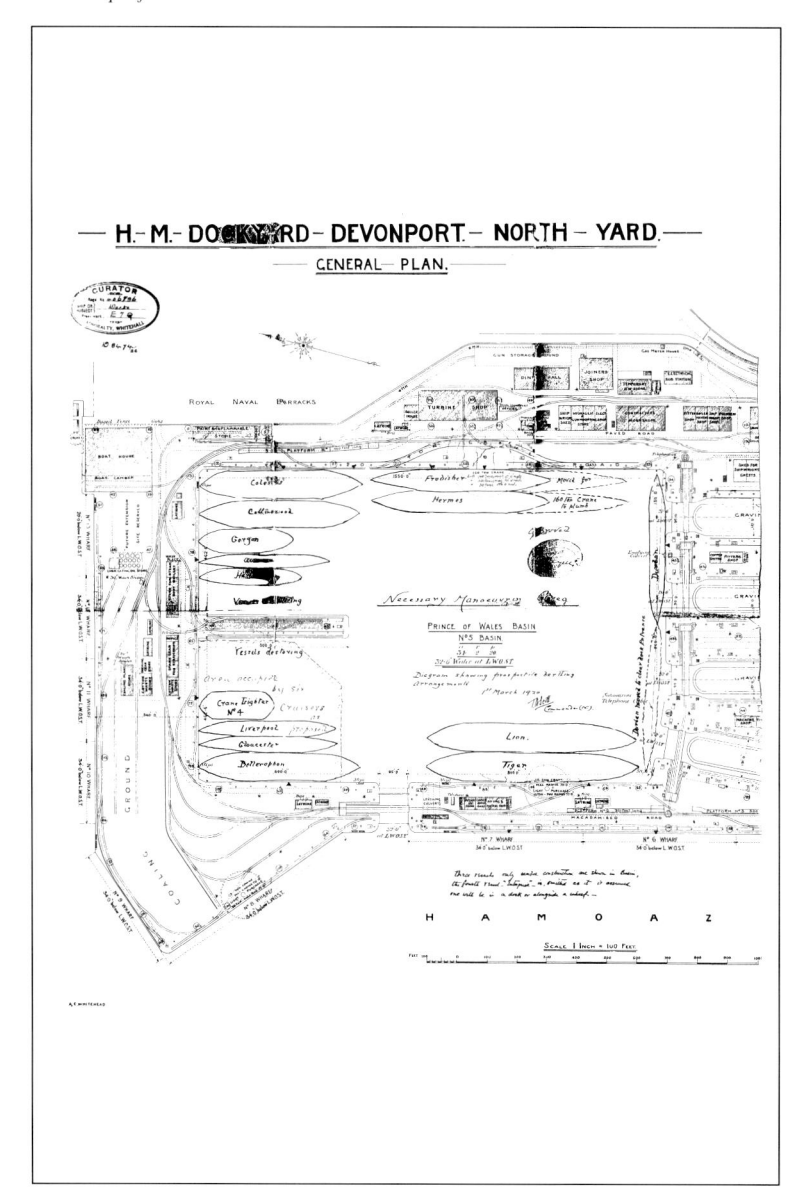

THE FIRST WORLD WAR

The great upsurge of traffic that the War brought about, indicated by the increase in workmen employed from 12,300 in 1914 to nearly 16,000 at the end of hostilities, plus the number of servicemen that inevitably passed through the establishment, sorely tried the capability of the existing facilities, and during the conflict more engine power was brought to Devonport. In the period between 1914 and 1919, eight new locomotives arrived. Having had a spell of exclusively ordering from Hawthorn Leslie - five in a row - the Yard turned elsewhere, and only two of the eight were from them. Of the remainder one was from Avonside Engineering at Bristol and the remainder were supplied by Andrew Barclay in Glasgow.

In the First World War alterations were made to the internal layout of tracks to allow troop trains to reach the north end of North Yard and platforms were built at a cost of £8,000. The platforms, each of about 400 feet in length, were built during April and May 1915 around 5 Basin, and curves were eased to 300 feet radius. It was anticipated that 12 trains a day of 900 feet each could then be handled, at the rate of two trains every three hours in a working day of 18 hours. Some indication of the usage of these platforms is gained from instructions on the handling of horses arriving by train issued in June 1915. Water troughs were provided and at 6 wharf a rail for tethering 100 horses. Troops returning from combat required Hospital trains, and these also used the platforms, but were followed by a water tank wagon from which disinfectant was sprayed onto the track.

Not all went well. The GWR wrote to the War Office on 12 January 1916 to complain that four trains carrying troops for embarkation were seriously delayed due to the opening of a caisson between 8 a.m. and 11.40 a.m. Congestion was rife. In December 1915 780 trucks belonging to the main line companies were stuck in the Yard, the lack of engine power together with other traffic and the intricacy of the Dockyard railway system being blamed. By the end of January the following year the number of trucks held up had been reduced to 177. The GWR were asked to loan engines, to further reduce this, but the request 'could not be considered in the prevailing circumstances'. In the first two years of the War 65,000 trucks had been dealt with, and it is no wonder that extra locomotives were sought.

As a precaution in the event of Zeppelin airship raids, the Dockyard fire engines were stationed in the tunnel entrances for protection. At the giving of an alert the passenger train rolling stock was to be

Admiral Superintendent's Memos relating to the railway in the period 1902 to 1925.

Admiral Superintendent's Memos relating to the railway in the period 1902 to 1925.

shunted onto the track to the north of No 7 dock and the locomotive returned to shed. In the event the air-raids were confined to the North Sea coast so these arrangements were never required.

With nearly all the Yard a densely built-up industrial area, the possibility of the steam locomotives starting fires is remote, but in Gun Wharf it was a different matter with extensive grass covered banks on either side of the line. One bad day for the Yard was 20 June 1921 when sparks from an engine caused the grass banks of the Gun Wharf cutting to ignite and burn some railings. This was not in itself a major problem but at the same time the Hemp Store in South Yard also caught fire. These unconnected events sorely tested the fire service.

The heavy usage of the passenger train had tragic results in 1932. The lack of sufficient room for the numbers of men travelling at certain times of the day resulted in considerable numbers riding by standing on the footboards of the carriages, in spite of notices forbidding the practice. However such practices persisted with fatal consequences. At just after midday on Friday 9 October 1932, the 12.05 p.m. train from Extension Yard left fully loaded, and with men riding on the steps outside the carriages. Approaching the Cantilever Crane the fireman, Tom Burley, looked back along the train and called out to those breaking the rules to get off. The train was estimated to be travelling at 6 m.p.h. A GWR road lorry was parked adjacent to the track and as the train passed one of those perched on the carriage steps, Robert Selley (a labourer), struck the lorry and was knocked to the ground. He died later of his injuries at the Royal Naval Hospital, Stonehouse. It was as a result of this incident that the sign illustrated on page 73, prohibiting such dangerous practices, was affixed to the carriage sides and a stern warning issued, that the running of services outside normal working hours (i.e. before 7.30 a.m. and after 4.00 p.m. and strictly not necessary) would cease.

Up until 1932 the Constructive Department of the Dockyard provided the signalmen and guards whilst the Engineering Department employed the drivers. However in this year responsibility transferred to the Stores Dept, where it remained until Devonport Management Ltd. took over the operation of the whole railway in 1993.

Ever increasing warship size required larger docks and in 1924 the entrance to No 5 Basin was widened to 125 feet. Some four years later the first proposals were made for an equivalent increase of No 10 Dock from 95 feet, however it was not until 1936 that the work was begun. Between May 1937 and May

1940 Edmund Nuttall, Sons & Co. (London) Ltd., contractors, were engaged on the works, and to keep the inconvenience to the crowded dockyard to a minimum, a central concrete mixing plant was established. To move the wet concrete to the point of need, 2 cubic yard skips running on the standard gauge were hauled by two Ruston & Hornsby diesel locomotives. These were purchased new, and represented very early use of such units in industry. R&H works numbers 186314 and 186316 were supplied on 14 and 21 August 1937 respectively. They were 7 $1/2$ ton 44/48 BHP shunting locos fitted with electric starting and lights.

SECOND WORLD WAR AND AFTER

In preparation for the ensuing conflict, the water storage capacity for the Yards was increased by the construction of additional reservoirs. Messrs Bernard Sunley & Co. were awarded the contract and utilised a two foot gauge railway during construction, for which a collection of mining type locomotives was used.

Again the Second World War called for more engines and between 1939 and 1946 Andrew Barclay supplied three locomotives, to be numbered 17 and 18 and, strangely, number 2 was reused. The last steam locomotive arrived in 1950; the only time Bagnalls of Stafford supplied the Admiralty at Devonport.

The considerable damage suffered by Plymouth at the hands of the Luftwaffe also affected the dockyard railway. On the night of 25 August 1940, for example, one high-explosive bomb landed under the cantilever crane at the east of No 5 Basin causing damage to the line and sleepers. One of the big raids on Plymouth was during the night of 29 April 1941, and the tunnel received a hit, demolishing part of it and fatally injuring at least one of the Fire Watch party sheltering inside.

The social needs of the workforce were also considered and in August 1941 the Government introduced their scheme for Assisted Travel for Evacuated Workers. The Dockyard issued vouchers to those who had been forced to move out of the city and took up with the GWR instances of difficulties experienced. One such being that for those travelling on the 5.30 a.m. special service from Tavistock, but having to wait nearly half-an-hour at North Road Station for the connecting train to arrive at Keyham at 6.44 a.m.

A wartime mishap, not of the Germans' making, occurred at the North Yard loco shed in about 1941. A fitter working on a locomotive in steam opened the regulator without realising the engine was in forward gear, whereupon it accelerated through the buffers and demolished the rear wall of the shed, much to the shock of a crowd of 'Yardees' standing outside. The culprit reported sick for some time after. At this time the shed was staffed by one fitter, one boilermaker and two labourers, with an apprentice from time to time.

On page 17 is mentioned the 1860s extensions to Gun Wharf, including the narrow and broad gauge rail tracks constructed then. As late as the 1960s 18 inch gauge trackwork was indicated on plans connecting the riverside wharf to a store, with a branch under a gantry that also served a standard gauge track, allowing trans-shipment between the two systems.

Over the years the Dockyard has carried out sundry other work in connection with rail business. In September 1951 an 0-4-0ST Bagnall loco (Works No 2772 of 1944) was seen under repair in the Boiler Shop, this was from the Admiralty establishment at Llangennech, near Llanelly, in south Wales.

One incident occurred in the 1950s which fortunately did not result in personal injury, but which could have been far worse. The normal caisson at the entrance to No 5 Basin was out of service, and its replacement was in an offset position. The points were properly set for the rails over the temporary caisson, but the loco jumped the rails and ended up half over the edge of the basin. The driver was stranded in his cab until wire hawsers were put to the nearby capstans to haul the loco back. Another mishap was when a rail

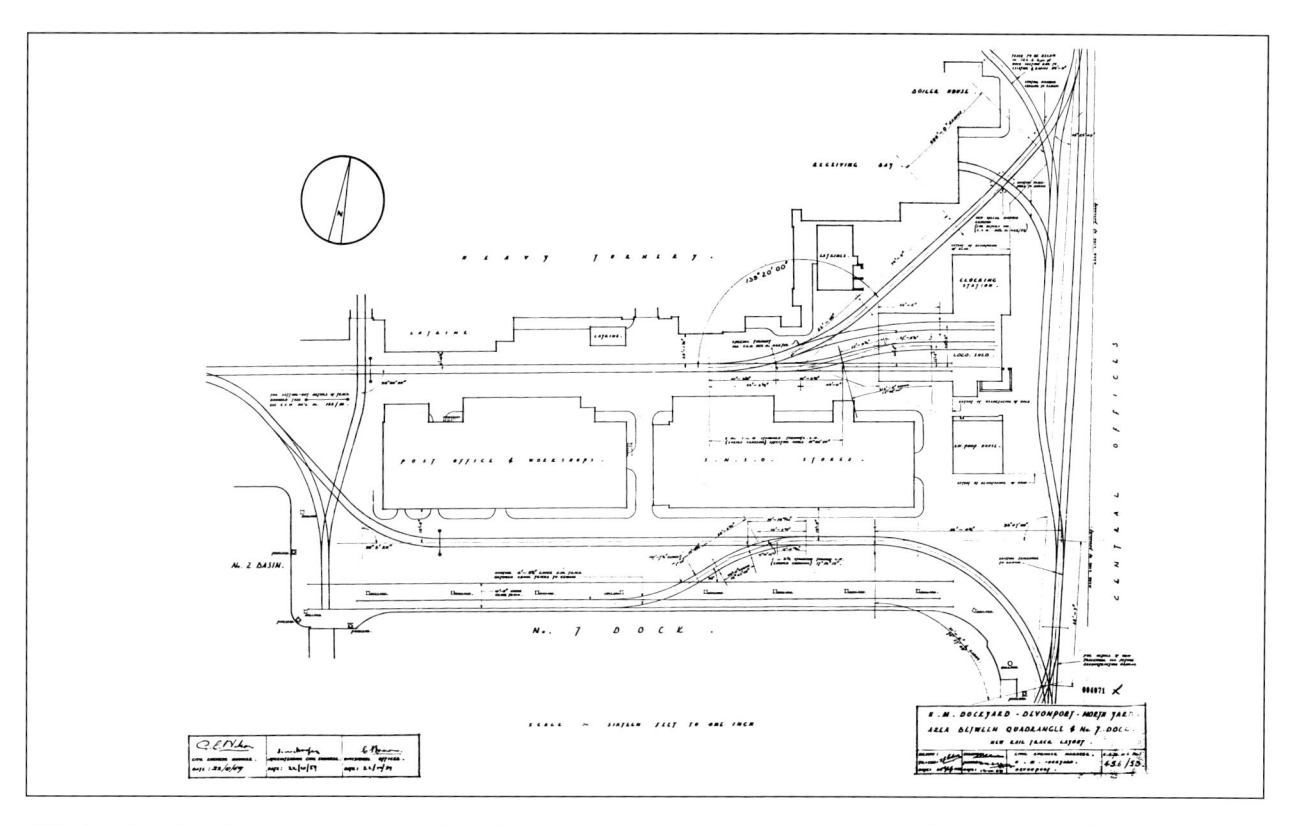

1959 Plan of the North Yard loco shed and area

crane collided with the passenger train. It transpired that the posted 'lookout' did not see the developing incident as he had only one eye.

One lark (of the many) involving apprentices was when some decided to play a trick on a very officious guard. An early morning train was standing on the loop at Central Offices when the boys uncoupled the last coach where this guard was sitting. He leant out of the window, gave the right-away to the driver, and sat back only to realise when it was too late that he had been left behind.

In 1955 the Admiralty ordered ten new diesels from F. C. Hibberd of London, carrying their trade name PLANET which increased the motive-power fleet dramatically. The steam locomotives remaining were gradually put out of operation, though good use was made of some of them by using them as stationary steam boilers.

In 1964 the new commercial television station serving the south west, Westward Television, made a half-hour documentary about the Dockyard. The opening scenes show the passenger service train and freight movements heading to South Yard. However greater film stardom was to come, of which more later.

The role of the railway, and the passenger train, had been to provide a link between the physically separate Yards that comprise Devonport Dockyard. However the rise in road vehicle use after the Second War led to the conclusion that there had to be a road link provided. In the early 1960s two road bridges were built, from South to Morice Yards across Cornwall Beach and Morice to North Yards over the Torpoint Ferry approach road. This signalled the demise of the passenger train and the final day of normal working of the service was Friday 13 May 1966. However the very last run was performed with some ceremony on the following Monday at 10.30 a.m. from South Yard, with (the second) No 2 specially steamed for the event. Driver Alex Lambie was at the controls, with some exalted footplate visitors; the Captain of the Dockyard Capt. W. J. M. 'Jasper' Teal and the Superintending Naval Stores Officer Mr F. N. Carter. The train had been decorated with flags and all the conventions of the carriage class distinctions were forgotten for this final run and anyone was allowed in the compartments. No 2 carried the Royal Coat of Arms that had been borne by the loco No 1 up to its scrapping in 1949. A replacement bus service came into operation that day, and still runs.

Despite this apparent major reduction in rail facilities that the withdrawal of the passenger train would indicate, more improvements were implemented. Around the heads of No 5, No 6 and No 8 Docks in North Yard track relaying of track with 109 lb. per yard dock rail was carried out in 1966 and 1967. South Yard saw further rail alterations and renewals in the period 1967 to 1969 in the vicinity of No 3 Slip.

At the end of June 1970 a new £100,000 workshop for the Yard Services Dept. was opened in South Yard, with full facilities for the maintenance of railway engines. In 1971 a new Pipe Shop was designed to stand where the old Gunmounting Shop was located, immediately next to the Exchange Sidings. This necessitated alterations to the sidings in 1972 by moving them to the east by some 20 feet. The bank adjacent to the wall next to Saltash Road was cut into and a retaining wall built to create sufficient space. The sidings area, previously sleepered and ballasted track, was now relaid in concrete with the tracks level with the hardstanding to create additional transit capability. A weighbridge was included, with rails in the deck, but these were never connected to the system, and remain so to this day. One result of this development was to change the normal rail access to the northern end of North Yard. The single track 'main line' to the east of the Gunmounting shop was taken out of use and lifted before the new Pipe Shop construction commenced, and new line to the south and west of the new building, laid with a sharp reverse curve, remained the only route north.

DECLINE, BUT NOT DEMISE

Grand developments were planned in 1977, with a streamlining of the railway. Some areas in North Yard would have lost their rail tracks but a smoothing out of some of the

1952 Survey of the tunnel, with clearances and speed information.

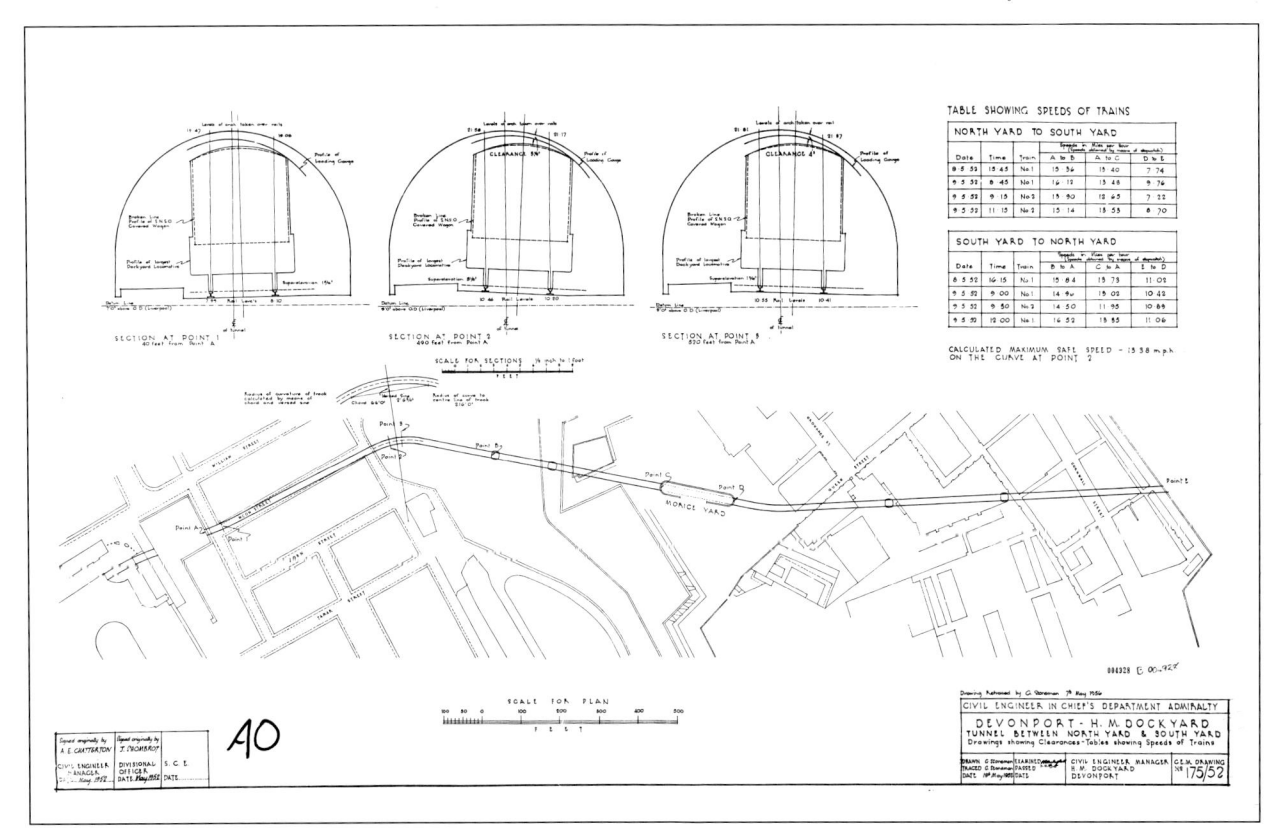

The internal freight service survived into the 1980s. In November 1980 driver Dave Rogers (in cab) assisted by Derek Edwards, with a short train, complete with the guards van.
DAVE ROGERS COLLECTION

The 'cresting' of class 50, number 50032, COURAGEOUS adjacent to Drake Platform on Saturday 11 October 1986, by the wife of Capt. Niall Kilgour, the CO of the submarine of the same name. This event was nearly thwarted as a trial clearance run on 25 September, with 50006, raised concerns over whether the class was permitted on the branch.
N KILGOUR

sharper curves on the trunk lines would have resulted in major building demolition. Also the retention of most of the facilities in Morice and South Yards was proposed. However none of this work came to fruition, although one development of this period did result in some new tracks being laid. This was the new facility specially built for the upkeep of the Royal Navy's nuclear submarine fleet, completed in 1982. New rails were laid into the complex and were first tested on 20 February 1979, by locomotive Yard No 5199.

The one occasion that the Dockyard Railway has achieved star status was in the Columbia Pictures film made in 1978, entitled 'Force Ten from Navarone'. In February of that year the film team and the starring cast, including Robert Shaw, Harrison Ford and Edward Fox, used the area around the South Smithery as a wartime location depicting a port in Yugoslavia under German control. One of the Planet locos, driven by Clifford Whitrow, and a rake of BR and Dockyard trucks played a large part. The loco carried a German swastika but the truck numbers appeared in the background, to the great amusement in subsequent years of those in the know. At the end of the ten minute sequence the actors climbed into one of the trucks, and the train headed north towards the tunnel... to emerge into the Yugoslav hills.

Mishaps continued, as can be expected on any such congested industrial railway. At about 8.30 on the morning of Friday, 4 June 1982, British Rail brought to Keyham a closed van, VDA No 201000, from Park Royal. At this time the procedure was for arriving wagons to be left secured on their brakes on the branch at Keyham, where-upon the Dockyard loco would come up the branch to collect them. As the main line engine was uncoupled, the wagon immediately started to roll down the 1 in 70 gradient. A warning was telephoned through to the Exchange Sidings and the driver of the Dockyard locomotive No 5200 attempted to move to match the speed of the truck, but was too late. The impact caused the loco to be moved 109 feet, shearing every bolt on the chassis and it was subsequently sold off as 'beyond economic repair'. Fortunately the driver did not suffer too much from his ordeal. The cause of the accident was established as faulty brakes on the truck. Needless to say the practice of BR leaving trucks at Keyham was hastily revised. The Dockyard engines would be ready to meet incoming trains there or BR delivered them to the Sidings.

A ceremonial duty on the branch occurred on Saturday 11 October 1986. The nuclear powered submarine *HMS Courageous* was re-

Rail services to South Yard ceased on 10 November 1982, with the closure of the tunnel. The last passage through was Hibberd Planet loco Yard No. 4860 suitably decorated, seen here on arrival in North Yard. PLYMOUTH NAVAL BASE MUSEUM

dedicated after a two year refit in the Dockyard, and after lunch the Network South East Class 50 locomotive of the same name (running number 50 032) was 'crested' adjacent to the Platform in HMS Drake. This involved the unveiling of the ship's crest, which was attached to the side of the locomotive. The wife of Captain N. S. R. Kilgour RN (then Commanding Officer of the submarine) performed the ceremony before a small audience.

The run down of the railway became apparent when, on 10 November 1982, the last rail movement through the tunnel was worked. Driver Dave Rogers was at the controls of No 4860 and Jim Leach was assistant driver. The locomotive was suitably decorated with flags and carried a headboard commemorating the event. It left light engine from South Yard at 12.05 p.m. to be met by the Port Admiral, Vice Admiral David Brown, on arrival at North Yard at 12.20. A crowd of spectators gathered to see the last train staff handed ceremoniously over. This is now mounted on display in the Plymouth Naval Base Museum.

The last development in connection with conventional rail freight movements was the laying of an additional siding 94 metres long (number four) to the east of the Exchange Sidings in 1982, although the proposed construction of a transit shed on this line was never proceeded with.

A most unusual operation on the section of the railway passing through the Barracks occurred in the latter years when the Captain

Driver Dave Rogers (in bowler hat!) hands over the train staff to Vice Admiral David Brown on 10 November 1982, after the last movement through the tunnel. PLYMOUTH NAVAL BASE MUSEUM

of HMS Drake left his post. A 'tradition' was started whereby he was conveyed away from the Barracks Platform in the railway brakevan, which was suitably dressed in flags and bunting. On at least one occasion the driver had to keep pace with a band marching along the adjacent road. This event became a little difficult after the brakevan had been sold but improvisation in 1992 resulted in Captain Wixon travelling on a platelayers' trolley, covered to disguise its humble origins, loaned by Grant Lyon Eagre (a contractor undertaking refurbishment work on the railway at the time).

THE DOCKYARD PRIVATISED

The Government of the 1980s embarked on a policy of privatising various state operations. The Dockyards at Rosyth and Devonport were 'Contractorised' in April 1987 and Devonport became operated by Devonport Management Ltd., a joint venture company owned by three major industrial businesses. The result of this move has been the seeking, and winning, of commercial non-Naval work on a scale not previously seen in the Yard, and railway work has been a ready source of contracts.

In 1990, between May and October, a contract was secured from BR to overhaul electrical systems of 14 coaches in the Intercity fleet, and a driving trailer was also seen here.

Another very successful project has been the overhaul of Paxman diesel engine units from HST power cars, over 100 having been completed by 1993. These engine blocks are removed from the rolling stock and brought by road. The intention to undertake further similar work to classes 37 and 47 locomotives resulted in a single trial order for one engine. To conduct the running trials an accident damaged class 47, number 47538, was loaned to the Yard in October 1991. This arrived by rail from Penzance where it had suffered an end-on collision. Once the trial had been completed the engine-less loco stood in the Exchange sidings until 17 February 1993 when it was removed to Crewe on a large road low loader. The loco was propelled onto the truck by Yard engines 4858 and 4860, and in fact this was the last movement under their own power of these two veterans, before

One of the more bizarre uses of a railway. The departure of the Commanding Officer of HMS Drake, Capt. Wixon in March 1992, upon relinquishing his command. With his wife he was hauled from Drake Platform to the Car Park Crossing by his senior officers upon a (suitably concealed) borrowed platelayers trolley.
COLLECTION P. BURKHALTER

Devonport Management Ltd. has entered the railway engineering business as part of the diversification to offset defence reductions. Here on 20 October 1990 is driving trailer 9711 for works. Ironically 9711 was the number of the regular 0-6-0PT locomotive in steam days that worked into the Dockyard on transfer freights.
DEVONPORT MANAGEMENT LTD.

being placed out of use.

The reason for the Planet diesels' demise was the need to air-brake trains, and the Ministry of Defence arranged the transfer of two Drewry diesel locomotives from the Army Rail Organisation in March 1993.

Devonport Management Limited took over the entire management of the railway on 4 October 1993.

The Yard had to wait until 1993 to enjoy the privilege of having a main line locomotive carry its name, although all their own always sported the name. InterCity power car 43181 was named *Devonport Royal Dockyard 1693-1993* at a ceremony at Plymouth Station on Thursday 25 November 1993. At 9.15 a.m. on Platform 4, the Flag Officer Plymouth, Vice-Admiral Sir Roy Newman KCB, unveiled the nameplate to a fanfare of Marine trumpeters. Also in attendance were Lady Newman, Mr Mike Leece (then Managing Director of Devonport Management Ltd.) and Mrs Leece, plus other representatives of the Navy and many of the civilian organisations supporting the Base, including this author. Employees of DML involved in the HST diesel engine re-fitting project attended and it was suitably appropriate that the Paxman diesel engine in the locomotive was one that had been overhauled by the Company. The party was entertained to breakfast aboard the train hauled by 43181, which formed the 9.35 a.m. Plymouth to Paddington train. It was arranged that the tail locomotive on this service was 43188 *City of Plymouth*. The party returned from Exeter on the 11.17 a.m. ex-Leeds. At Exeter replica nameboards were

In recognition of the tricentenary of Devonport Dockyard, HST power car, class 43 number 181, was named by Rear Admiral Sir Roy Newman, at Plymouth Station on 25 November 1993. Here with Sir Roy, are Brian Scott MD InterCity GW and Mike Leece, then MD DML.
COLLECTION P. BURKHALTER

On a very wet January morning in 1994, the first HST set slowly moves onto the branch at Keyham Junction.
LOU WATKINS

presented to both Admiral Newman and Mr Leece.

Devonport Management Ltd., in conjunction with ABB the large multi-national railway engineers, successfully secured a contract in 1993 with BR InterCity to fit a secondary door locking system to the fleet of High Speed Train sets based in the west country. The contract requirement was for an eight coach set to be installed with the equipment in a one week timescale. The only place available to undertake this work was at the Exchange Sidings and at the end of 1993 scaffold train covers were erected over one track to enable the work to proceed protected from the elements. However both the run-round facility at Keyham Station and the loops in the exchange sidings were shorter than the HST set. Furthermore InterCity could not spare the power cars with which the sets were normally coupled to remain unused for a week. As a result the sets were moved from Laira depot to the Dockyard with a barrier coach at each end, and with a class 47 locomotive at one end and a class 08 shunting engine at the other. A complicated shunting manoeuvre in the exchange sidings was necessary to release both locomotives. The huge formation was moved each Friday evening during 1994, but with the first special arriving on Tuesday 4 January. The contract came to a successful conclusion on 24 February 1995 after a total of 1,845 coaches had been converted at Devonport. On this last day the Dockyard to Laira movement was performed by 47816 and 08645.

The 350hp class 08 shunter had the task of moving the ten coach train on the 1 in 70 gradient, which on one occasion in very wet weather has proved beyond its capability. On 19 August 1994 08648 had to be banked out of the sidings by both the Dockyard Drewry shunting engines. It was during one of the regular Friday evening changeovers that a mishap occurred, the first for many years. On 25 November 1994 Class 47 BR locomotive (number 47832) derailed at the north end of the Exchange sidings, one bogie ending up on the ballast. The Laira recovery team were quickly on the scene and within two hours had the locomotive back on the rails, with no signs of damage to either track or engine.

Prior to the commencement by Devonport Management Ltd. of the contract to fit secondary door locks to HST coaches, a clearance trial was conducted on Sunday 23 May 1993. This unusual view, from a high lift platform, shows the southern end of the Exchange Sidings, with the HST standing on track 1.
DEVONPORT MANAGEMENT LTD.

A brighter day in February 1995 saw the departure of the final HST train, here passing the platform in HMS Drake.
P. BURKHALTER

THE FUTURE

In the summer of 1993 the Government decided to construct facilities at Devonport for the re-fitting of the Trident nuclear submarine fleet. This decision secures the long-term future of the Dockyard well into the twenty-first century, as well as ensuring that the railway will also see activity in the long term in support of the nuclear work. Scheduled for completion early in the next century, the new facilities require new trackwork to be laid within North Yard as an integral part of dealing with the work involved in the nuclear fleet overhauls.

CHAPTER SEVEN

THE PASSENGER TRAIN SERVICE

No exact recorded details of the first running of a train service specifically for passengers has yet been discovered. However when considering the design of the Barracks in 1883 it was recognised that the distance between that establishment and the hub of operations then in South Yard, would require the provision of 'third class carriages' on the railway. What is certain is that by August 1897 a scheduled passenger service had commenced from the Barracks Platform, the destination of which is not stated, but must be assumed to be South Yard. The Barracks were first occupied in June 1889, by 500 men, so it is possible that the train service dates from then. Whether any arrangements for the conveyance of passengers, either formally or informally, existed before this time is not known but, if later events were anything to go by, riding on goods trains was not unknown. There was at this time a sharp increase in employment levels in the Dockyard, from 5,200 in 1890 to 9,500 in 1910, which coincided with the expansion of the Yard to the north.

A newspaper report recorded that on 12 October 1899 a collision between the passenger train and some badly stacked machinery caused the officer's coach to be damaged to the extent that it had to be removed from service for repair.

The rapid growth of the Dockyard in the early part of the twentieth century also coincided with the arrival in 1902 of a very forward looking Admiral Superintendent (the Dockyard's Chief Officer), one Rear Admiral W. H. Henderson. He brought to the Yard all manner of reforms, only some of which concern this particular story. Of associated interest was the introduction of scheduled passenger steamboats plying up and down the river, specifically for Naval personnel, calling at landing stages and boats moored in the river. He also observed that a large number of men were passing through the tunnel on foot and instigated a check on the necessity of this. The net result was the almost instantaneous reduction sevenfold of this movement. One significant initiative during his tenure between 1902 and 1906 was the formalising of

On display in the Plymouth Naval Base Museum are the class designation plates that were fixed to the carriage doors.
P. BURKHALTER

On arrival at North Yard, March 1963. The locomotive (No 18) is about to run-around the stock using the crossover in the foreground. The track layout is still extant and in use in 1996. B MILLS

The passenger train c 1960, at South Yard terminus. The four rear carriages were for workmen, and the front two for higher ranks. This was the standard train arrangement. COLLECTION P. BURKHALTER

the passenger train service into a regular interval operation.

On Henderson's arrival he found that the service ran at an average interval of 1 hour 5 minutes, with nine trains in working hours for men and materials, plus two outside working hours for men only, presumably immediately before and after the day shift. Seven of the eleven trains ran through to the Barracks platform but the others were from one end of the tunnel to the other, that is, South Yard to Central Offices. The extended service to the Barracks was necessary as, until the completion of the Extension Works in 1907, the majority of ships were in South Yard. Henderson's initiative in 1902 was to direct that the trains should run to a regular 20 minute interval service, to avoid the standing around waiting that occurred without the existence of a defined timetable.

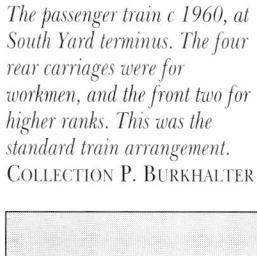

To further reduce the workforce needlessly travelling around the Yard a railway mail service was introduced in January 1902. Mail boxes were placed adjacent to the train's stopping places in each Yard, where items for transfer could be placed. The train Guard was responsible for clearing the box and carrying the contents to the other terminus, where messengers would collect it. A more regularised service was introduced on 11 May 1903, when specified trains were to carry the mail, on the hour from 8 a.m. to 5 p.m. from Devonport, and at 5 minutes past the hour from Keyham.

On completion of the Extension works in 1907 the service through the tunnel was extended to the northern end of the new Yard, diverting from the Barracks. The extended distance meant that the service evolved into a half-hourly interval service, extending from beside No 5 basin to the head of the South Yard Camber. Intermediate stops were made at Cantilever, North Yard, Central Offices and Morice Yard, the journey taking about 20 minutes. Towards the end of the First World War nearly 16,000 men were employed in the Dockyard and two sets of rolling stock were in use, with (usually) dedicated crews and locomotives. The latter in the first half of this century were Nos 1 and 2, although once the diesel locomotives arrived none were specifically allocated.

The first passenger service ran just before 7 a.m. and around 20 half hourly trains ran during the day, Monday to Friday, up to 5 p.m. There was a short break in service at lunchtime. On a Friday afternoon the Yard finished slightly earlier so the service was truncated, with the opportunity taken to clean the coaches. The two trains crossed in front of the Central Offices, although it is reported that if one was running late - or conversely, early - the crossing could be effected at St Levans. Both rakes of coaches were stabled at Central Offices when not in service, hence each days' services commenced or terminated here. In 1964 the annual cost of running the passenger train service was £14,105.

Full details of the carriages are contained in the Rolling Stock chapter.

It depended on each Admiral Superintendent (they changed every two years or so) as to whether they would travel by train from their residence in South Yard to Central Offices. At the times when they did, in the morning, lunchtime and afternoon, the guard would unlock the compartment, switch on the lights and salute the Admiral on board.

A survey of the train service usage in 1964 has survived, and for the journey through the tunnel at no time were less than 20 carried. At the morning and lunch peaks, around 100 were on board, but it was the 4.05 p.m. northbound service from South Yard which saw almost the full capacity used when 153 travelled.

At one end of the train was marshalled a flat truck, provided for the tool boxes that accompanied the tradesmen, plus sundry materials which were being carried by passengers. The aforementioned survey provides an interesting list of the goods carried:

Asbestos sheeting, batteries, bicycle, castings, copper tube, coir rope, drillpost & hoses, dustbin, electric fire, felt, forgings, galvanised pipes, nuts & bolts, oil drum, overalls, paint, paraffin, plywood, pneumatic tools, sack truck, steel strip, tackles, timber trolley, timber, valves, washbasins, wheelbarrow, wire netting.

After the fatal accident in 1932, when someone riding on the steps outside the coach was killed, the rules relating to the use of the train were tightened up and on the coach sides was placed the following notice:

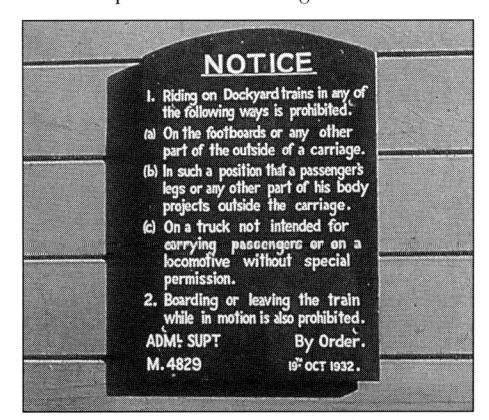

One coach on each train had this warning notice posted, issued as a result of a fatal accident in 1932 when a workman fell off a train.
P GRAY

As related earlier, the passenger service ceased on 13 May 1966.

The South Yard signalman looks on as the last passenger service runs on 13 May 1965, hauled by No 2 carrying the royal coat of arms.

Not all trains on the last day of the passenger service were steam hauled; here Yard No 4859 arrives in South Yard. Note the driver handing the single line staff over to the signalman.
PLYMOUTH NAVAL BASE MUSEUM

THE TRAIN CONVEYS ROYALTY

King Edward VII and Queen Alexandra were in Devonport for the launch of the battleship *HMS Queen* and the keel laying of *HMS King Edward VII* on Saturday 8 March 1902. Prior to the main ceremonies in the afternoon, the Royal Party travelled to the Royal Naval Barracks for the presentation of medals. For this purpose the Dockyard Train was positioned next to the Royal Yacht berthed alongside in Devonport Yard, and at 11.40 a.m. their Majesties boarded for the journey through the tunnel and to the Barracks Platform. A second ceremony at the Keyham Engineering College followed before the train conveyed the party back to the Yacht for lunch at 1.30 p.m. Locomotive No 1, only three years old at the time and under the charge of Driver R. R. H. Palk, was given the task of hauling the royal party. A royal crest was cast and, mounted on the lower side sheets of the locomotive cab, was carried for the rest of its working life. The crest, a commemorative plate and a photograph were mounted on a display board in the North Yard engine shed, and today they survive in the Plymouth Naval Base Museum.

Whilst on the subject of Royal Visits, it has often been mentioned that the Royal Train has at various times ventured onto the Dockyard Railway. This appears very plausible, and the author has endeavoured to trace exact instances. However all accessible records fail to include mention of any such visit, although that is not to say that such a visit has never taken place.

CHAPTER EIGHT
FREIGHT

The original reason for the railway in the Dockyard was to provide a means of conveying goods. The road vehicles available in the mid-nineteenth century were slow and of not great carrying capacity. Rail based wagons could convey much larger items. The first line to be laid in the yard was to haul ships' boilers from the workshop to the dockside crane for installation. The Yard would have had its own stock of trucks for internal use only, as well as taken deliveries in the main line companies' stock.

In the First World War the demand for coal for the Navy dramatically increased, and 2,500,000 tons in 13,600 trucks were shipped from South Wales to Devonport, instead of by sea as usual in peacetime. Indeed, the weight of materials arriving can be best judged from the size of the ships built at Devonport as the Navy moved from timber to steel with which to construct its fleet, from about 1885 onwards.

Weight of ships built

5 years ended	tonnage built	note
1875	9,000	1
1880	12,000	1
1885	12,000	1
1890	32,000	2
1895	64,000	2
1900	61,000	2
1905	87,000	2
1910	144,000	2

note 1: composite construction, i.e. iron frames with timber planking
note 2: wholly steel construction

The freight trains from the main line would comprise between 5 and 25 wagons, carrying anything from ordinary stores, through steel plate and cable drums on well trucks, to propellers, explosives and aviation fuel. Whole tree trunks arrived destined for the South Yard sawmill. Coke for the Yard boilers came by rail, but the coal for the ships arrived by sea at the coal tip. Torpedoes

On a southbound freight from Extension at the south end of the sidings, No.2 (the second) hauls internal wagons. C HORSHAM

In 1964 F Hibberd 'Planet' Yard number 4860 shunts loaded BR bogie wagons loaded with rough and prepared timber in South Yard.
C HORSHAM COLLECTION

arrived in trucks to the Torpedo Shop, adjacent to the Exchange sidings. The Cold Store on No 5 wharf received meat delivered in refrigerated trucks. The approach to the Cold Store was inconvenient, and two locomotives were required to place and remove the trucks on either side of a turntable. Despatches from the Dockyard included stores for military depots around the country and scrap metal.

The haulage of gun barrels would seem to have been a regular occurrence as indicated by a drawing received in June 1938. This drawing was of LNER truck diagrams 15933D and 15934D for carrying 16 inch and 14 inch barrels. These bogie well trucks with a bogie match truck had an all-up weight of 159 tons carried on a total of 14 axles and a total length of 90 feet 9 inches but were designed to turn 100 foot curves. They date from possibly before the First World War and were still listed in the records in 1966. These would have been for the barrels to be bought from the manufacturers, Vickers Armstrong, at Gateshead, for mounting on such warships as *HMS Warspite* and *HMS Royal Oak*.

The area now occupied by the Frigate Refit Complex was originally the docks for the submarine refit work. Items removed from the submarines would be loaded by the dockside cranes into trucks which would be hauled across the dock caissons and into the Heavy Turnery and Boilershop. The steam loco would work into the building but the results of this manoeuvre on the workshop occupants are not recorded.

However the restricted profile of the tunnel has required care, and as a result two loading gauges were installed on the easternmost track in the Exchange Sidings. One was a conventional structure, to main-line gauge dimensions, but the other was specially constructed in the Dockyard for the unique purpose of checking wagon loads to pass through the tunnel. As the gauge was much lower than that for main line rolling stock, it was hinged to the adjacent wall to enable it to be swung out of the way. It was adjustable because longer wagons had to have a further reduced loading gauge due to the sharp bend in the tunnel, to avoid striking the tunnel roof. A swinging lever calibrated against a quadrant was marked for various lengths of truck, and the movement of the lever to the appropriate measurement would move the gauge height. Steel plate would arrive from the main line laid at an angle on the truck. Should this be the wrong way for passage through the tunnel, the truck would be turned around a triangle of tracks, south of 81 Shop. The reason for this was that the top edge of the plate would catch on the arch at the sharp bend, so it had to face away (or east) to avoid this.

Runaways whilst shunting in the sidings were not infrequent. If let go on the gradient there, the wagons would end up running slowly towards the Narrows. Another of the Yard near-misses occurred post-war when two tankers loaded with aviation fuel were being worked down from Keyham by the Dockyard engine. The train began to run away, possibly due to greasy rails, the police at South Barrack Gate telephoned St Levans with a warning, and the traffic was stopped. Fortunately there was a clear road through the sidings and the train ended up in the Narrows with a very shaken crew on board. For this reason a brake van was acquired in 1979 and to allow its use in the tunnel the Joiners Shop reduced the height and removed the end vestibules.

On arrival in the Exchange Sidings, the incoming wagon would have the Dockyard name of its final destination chalked on the side. They were then sorted in the sidings into trains for each destination, and moved off quite rapidly in view of the demurrage charges levied by the main line companies if a truck was kept beyond a certain time.

Should an empty wagon be required at any location, a phone call to the rail traffic office would be necessary to arrange an appropriate truck. Outgoing freight was far less than incoming, and mainly comprised the de-storing of a ship, bound for inland stores depots.

In 1964 an average of 620 tons of incoming freight and 180 tons of outgoing were handled each week, the principal cargoes being timber, steel and cable. The tunnel has always been a restriction on distribution and 20 per cent of all trucks with stores for South Yard had to be sent to Extension for off-loading as they would not go through the tunnel, a locomotive being almost permanently on duty there for shunting. The number of trucks being dealt with each week had been steady since the 1950s at 135. This included runners which were empty wagons marshalled next to overhanging loads. The distribution of destinations was:

20% Extension for trans-shipment
40% North Yard
30% South Yard
10% Morice Yard

Demurrage charges were incurred on those trucks held longer than BR permitted. This was due to delays in off-loading, but also to the slow movement to South Yard due to fitting movements around the half-hourly passenger. After a full study the decision in

Details of an adjustable loading gauge, to measure and check bogie wagons for clearances on the tight curve in the tunnel.

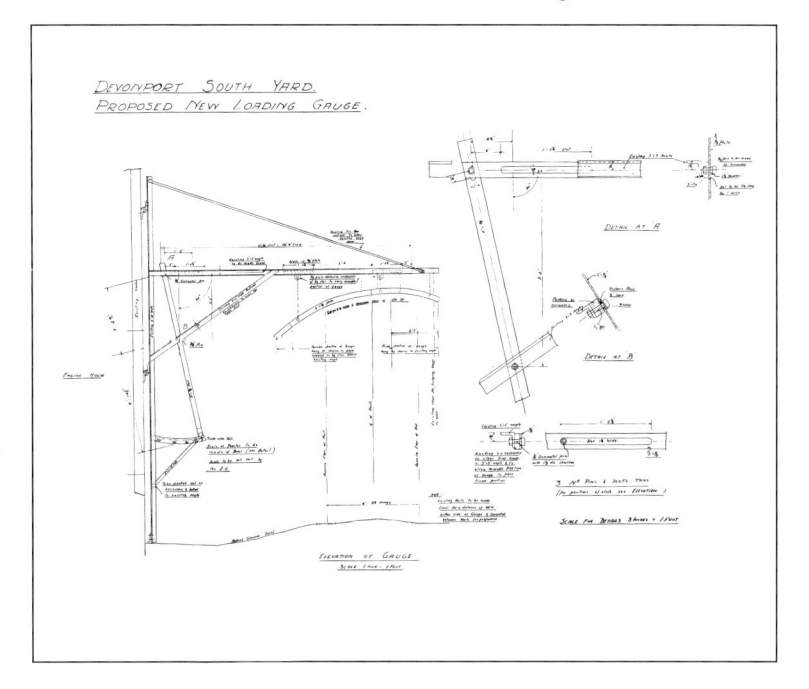

In 1961 Yard No 5199 shunts internal wagon 458 outside the ChainTest House, as can be surmised from the piles of chain links.
A ENDACOTT COLLECTION

1965 was to retain the rail freight service.

In 1976 it was reported that an average of 250 British Rail trucks passed through the Yard each month.

It all came under scrutiny again in 1981, and by then the Dockyard rolling stock comprised five locomotives and 20 internal trucks. Usage had declined to an average level of only one truck movement per day, but carrying the same type of materials as in 1964.

The costs of running the railway for these years have survived:

In the years 1978-1980, the railway staff, in addition to the drivers, were two signalmen, four shunters, three flagmen, and two supervisory grades.

The Falklands War of 1982 saw the last extensive use of the railway for freight, when large numbers of vans brought stores for loading on ships, including the *Atlantic Conveyor* which sailed on 25 April 1982 only to be later lost at sea. The movements were probably the most unusual to have been operated since the Second World War, and some detailed records of the extensive loads have survived:

Date	From	Time arr	Load
21.4.82	Thatcham	23.05	19 VDA vans
22.4.82	Thatcham	07.30	15 Ferry wagons
23.4.82	Long Marston	03.10	23 OBA wagons
23.4.82	Long Marston	14.25	12 wagons
31.5.82	Bicester	18.50	31 VDA vans

The last conventional freight movements recorded were in the closing months of 1984, although by this time they were reduced to very small loads.

The retention of the railway into the 1990s has been entirely due to the movement of waste from the refitting of nuclear submarines, which is taken to the reprocessing facilities at Sellafield, Cumbria. This commenced in May 1972, when a new, very large, purpose built rail transporter first arrived at Devonport for clearance testing.

	1978 £	1979 £	1980 £
BR demurrage	15,461	12,507	7,906
BR charges for the main line connection	3,200	3,500	3,900
Operating the railway (shunters, flagmen, clerks)	174,400	227,900	232,200
Track repair and maintenance	106,033	84,499	74,212
Locomotives, drivers & maintenance	54,852	62,479	77,624
Totalling	£353,946	£390,885	£395,842
These figures then permit the cost per movement to be calculated at:	£105.72	£152.63	£263.02

CHAPTER NINE

MAIN LINE SIGNALLING & BRANCH OPERATION

According to a report dated December 1868, prepared by the Cornwall Railway on the locking of the signals and switches at stations, the points for the Dockyard Branch at Keyham were protected by signals locked with the points. This was most probably by a early type of interlocking device and these signals would have been of the original disc and crossbar type as used on the GWR and its associates. This was the first signal on the Cornwall Railway to be detected by the facing points, that is, a very early form of safety interlocking.

The original system for controlling trains on the Cornwall Railway was by single needle telegraph instruments and crossing orders. The branch was in the Devonport to Saltash section. In succession to this earlier system, electric train staff equipment was installed between these points about 1892, and the ground frame for the Dockyard was then locked by Annett's key kept at Devonport. Most probably Annett's keys were attached to each train staff. However, by 1897 a full signal box had been opened at Keyham with a five lever frame. This was located immediately to the south of the road bridge on the down side. The ground frame still existed at that time, and it would seem that it was then released from the box, by a release lever.

The opening of the new double track main line as far as the approach to Weston Mill Viaduct in June 1900, and the opening of Keyham Station the next month, brought about the early demise of the original Keyham box. On 25 June 1900 the new box was opened, concurrently with the new double track main line, situated immediately adjacent to the northern end of the down platform. It contained 33 levers of which 25 were immediately in use. The new up platform loop opened in 1911 required the use of a total of 29 levers. June 1936 saw the installation of a 59 lever frame but, to save the expense of building a new box, a porch extension was added at the same time. The back loop was extended then to the physical limit that the road bridges at either end would permit and allowed trains of 49 wagons to be stabled, the work being funded by the Government Loan Scheme. A facing crossover between the up and down lines to the west of the junction facilitated the direct access to the branch. All this was shown on an illuminated diagram installed in the box.

THE ST BUDEAUX WARTIME CONNECTION

To the west of Weston Mill Viaduct the Great Western and the London & South Western ran parallel, a few yards apart and at similar levels. In the summer of 1919 a joint meeting between officials of the two companies examined the possibility of a connection from one to the other but as the GWR had only recently finished some new signalling work in the area they were reluctant to pay for more. So the matter rested until the Second War. All traffic for the Dockyard, and between there and the new Armament depot at Ernesettle, had to be routed via North Road station. With the risk of bombing on Plymouth it became apparent that an alternative route would be advisable. In September 1939 the GWR dusted off the 1919 plans and re-opened discussions with the Southern. Planning had reached an advanced stage in August 1940 when increasing air attacks on southern England brought matters to a head. The decision was made in September for the expenditure of

Keyham Signalling L Crosier

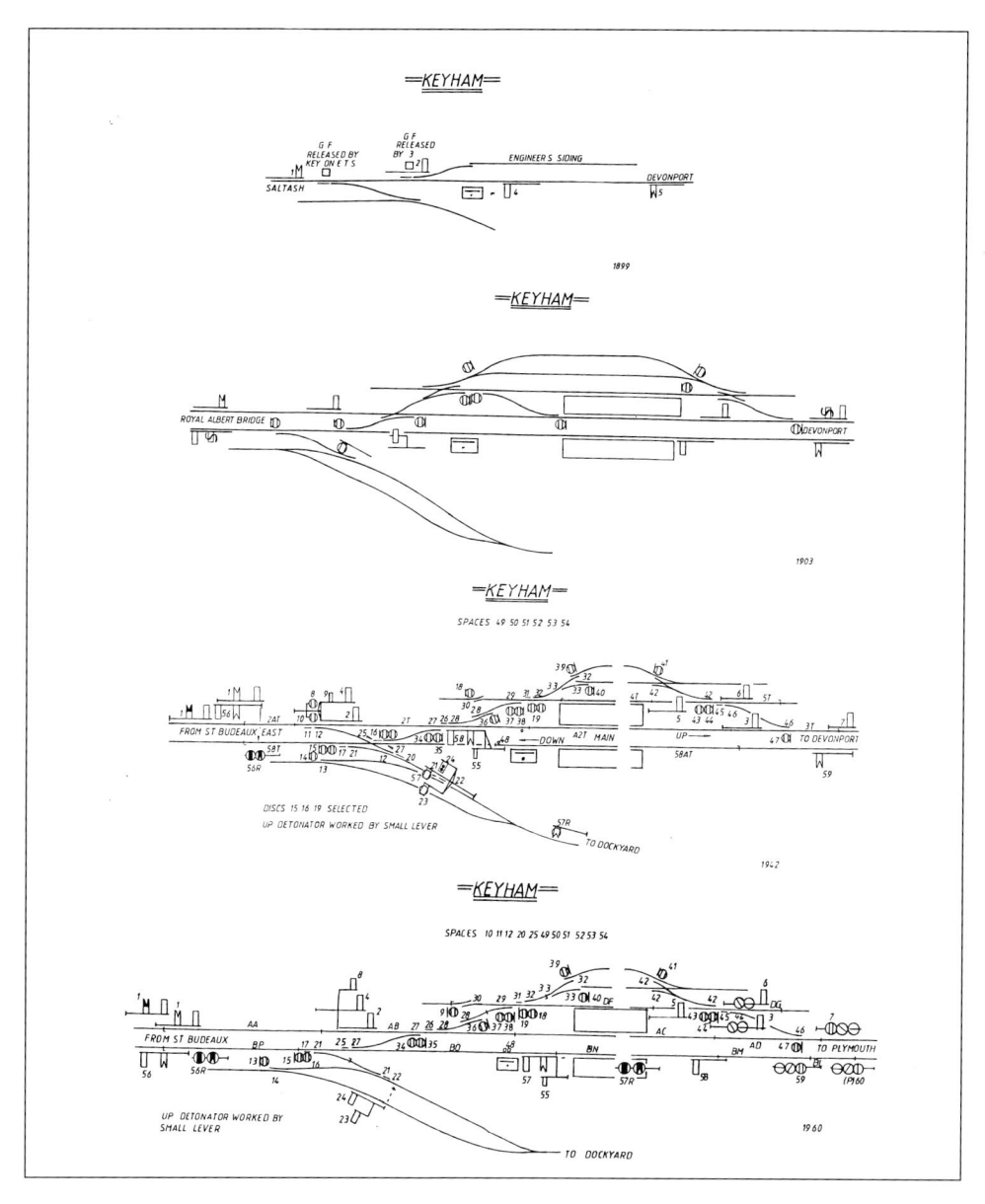

£14,000, and the SR was not long in starting work. New up sidings at St Budeaux (SR) were in operation on 12 January 1941, the idea being to have the extra capacity for trains waiting for acceptance by the Dockyard before crossing over to the GWR. The junction itself was commissioned on Sunday 2 March 1941, but full use had not been intended until the direct crossover to the Dockyard branch at Keyham Junction was brought into use on 23 May 1941. But events overtook this plan and heavy bombing of North Road Station on the night of 21 March saw all GWR services diverted over the connection and the SR to Exeter for two days. However from the end of May onwards all SR freights for the Dockyard ran directly from St Budeaux into the Yard and so relieved the congestion at North Road. Such was the pressure of the times that the Ministry of Transport Inspectors did not manage to visit the site and give approval until August 1946.

Ultimately the arrangement has survived. The section of SR line between St Budeaux and Devonport (Kings Road) was closed on 7 September 1964 the site of the St Budeaux wartime connection was restored for access to the line to Bere Alston and Gunnislake.

As a result of the rapid increase in traffic in the Second World War, and the resultant direct connection to the Southern at St Budeaux, there was installed a facing point from the up main leading direct onto the branch line by way of a crossover and single slip. This was intended to allow not only direct running into the Yard from the Southern but also gave the GWR a choice of using either the up or down lines for setting back onto the branch. The BoT reported the work as costing £2,500 and it was all brought into use on 23 May 1941.

The ending of hostilities and the resultant work involved in the restoration of normality elsewhere caused the wartime arrangements at Keyham to be left in until 1956. Two days before Christmas in that year the facing crossover was taken out of service and removed. Signalling modernisation arrived at Keyham on 2 July 1973, when the manual box closed and multiple aspect colour light signals installed operated from Plymouth Panel Box which controls all traffic from the west end of Totnes to St Germans. The entry to the Dockyard branch is currently controlled by a seven lever ground frame, called Keyham West. This also works the points to the west end of Keyham Loop and the crossover from down to up main lines. Shunt signal P164 controls the exit from the branch. Keyham East ground frame works the other end of the loop but is rarely used.

From the original annuity in the 1865 agreement has stemmed the continuing obligation for the Dockyard to pay the railway company for the cost of keeping the branch connection in operation. For example, from 1 January 1958 the working expenses were calculated as based on one Signalman's turn of duty, and were 8/40ths of one third of the annual cost of the Signal Box. This calculation would seem to be, firstly, due to the branch being only open during the day and, secondly, the number of levers in the box wholly necessary for accessing the branch as a proportion of the whole. The same formula was used in 1992 but based on the Panel Box at Plymouth.

Telephones were provided on the platform at the Barracks to call Keyham Signal Box. In later years a 'garden shed' was provided in the cutting near to the junction for the Dockyard Shunter and labelled Camels Head Signal Box. This building had three telephones, one to Keyham Box, one to the Exchange sidings and one to call the Captain's House in the Barracks to request the closure of the level crossing gates there.

Very detailed instructions have existed for the working of the branch by the main line companies. Over the years these were not much changed, so it can be surmised that they confirmed the working practices of earlier years. Here we examine the British Railways (Western Region) Sectional Appendix for

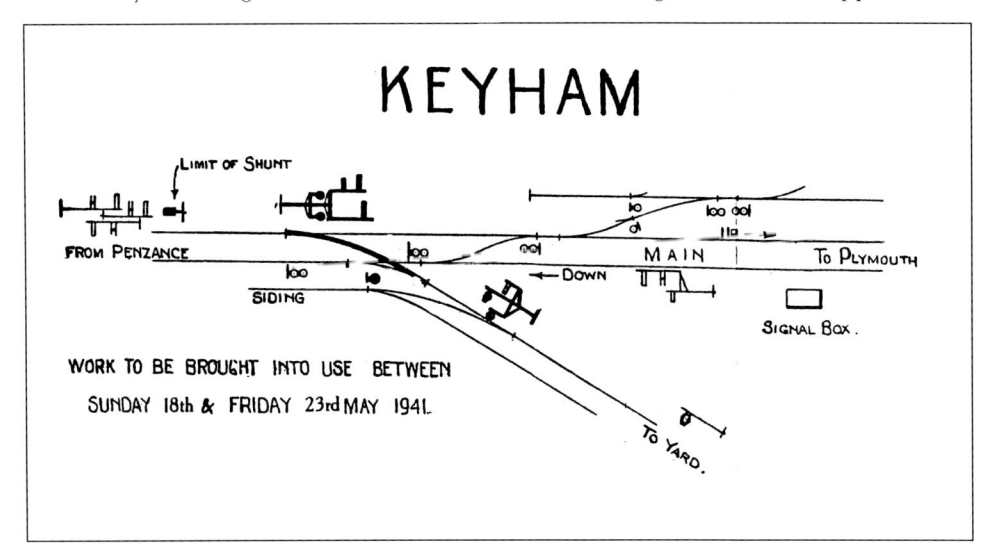

The additional main-line connections at St Budeaux and Keyham that were necessary in World War Two were detailed in these 1941 instructions.

June 1960. An earlier Great Western document is almost word for word the same.

Two pages of 15 detailed paragraphs cover all aspects of the mode of operation, which in summary were:

1. The Railways must make prior arrangements for warning the Dockyard of incoming traffic by phoning, so that the gates can be opened and the train staff brought to Keyham Junction. However it was guaranteed by the Yard to have a man at Keyham six mornings a week from 9 a.m. to 1.45 p.m. (12 noon on Saturdays) so as to receive the scheduled transfer freights.

2. Described the train staff, viz: being wooden suitably lettered, and that the section was between the Barrack Gates and the exchange sidings.

3. Forbade movements down the branch without the staff, but should the gates be closed then two engines could be stabled between there and the main line.

4 & 5. Dealt with the length of trains to be worked, and generally required all to be hauled down the branch. This meant that locomotives had to run round the train on the loop at the top of the branch. This limited trains to 16 four wheel wagons.

6, 7 & 8. The working of special passenger trains has always been a feature of the branch, and here were detailed instructions for their operation. Basically nine coach inbound loaded trains for the Barracks platform were backed from the down main onto the branch. However for such trains to go all the way to the Yard they had to be hauled and an extra engine was to be provided to replace the train engine to pull the set forward so that the train engine could be re-attached to the rear and then haul down the branch. All these were worked in reverse for outgoing trains.

9. Incoming special passenger services were to be advised to Keyham.

10. Freight trains were to be formed in the Dockyard Sidings before despatch.

11. Maximum loads for a passenger train to the Yard was 15 coaches, and a freight train 35 wagons and a brake.

12. Locations of telephones defined at the siding Offices and the Barracks Platform.

13. Engines not permitted to work over the line were those of King class and 47XX heavy freight class. All others could only go as far as sufficient to run around the train in the Exchange sidings.

14. Coaches less than 63 feet 6 inches were allowed to run onto the Dockyard lines as far as No 5 wharf, via the north side of No 5 basin.

For contrast the full London & South Western Railway Instructions for 1919 are reproduced at Appendix Four.

In the later years the rules were much simplified, to four simple paragraphs that exist at the time of writing, to reflect the dramatic decrease in freight after BR's cessation of the small load freight service. But the basics remain the same and there is still a large wooden staff in use for the single line from Keyham. The practice has been for the BR engine to draw the train to a stand on the down main line beyond the shunt signal, west of the branch junction. The train is then propelled across the crossover into Keyham station loop platform line where the locomotive can run around the stock. Once again the propelling movement is out to the down main line but with the locomotive at the head of the train to haul into the Yard. The Dockyard shunter is picked up before the gates into the Barracks and he hands the staff to the BR driver whilst conducting the train down the branch. The staff remains in the possession of the driver until return to Keyham, when the shunter and staff are dropped before returning to BR metals. Once again the run around movement is carried out before setting off eastwards.

As can be seen this whole operation brings the West of England line to a standstill, and has caused some grey hairs at times. The ground frame at Keyham West sees little use between movements, and can be a little stiff as a result. In one instance in 1993 it managed to seize up completely with the crossover set, and only the combined weight of the Dockyard shunter and BR signalman heaving on the levers managed to free off the reluctant rodding.

CHAPTER TEN
INTERNAL SIGNALLING & OPERATION

We have no detail of early practices of internal signalling, but we can deduce that as the Cornwall Railway installed the line through the Tunnel into South Yard in late 1876, then some form of train control would have been instigated by them at that time. From the evidence at the inquest into the tunnel fatality in July 1907, the following bell signals are surmised:

Bell (strokes)	Meaning
One sent	Are you there?
One received	Yes, I'm here
Two sent	Is tunnel clear?
Two received	Tunnel is clear
Continuous	NO
Three sent	Ordinary train coming
Three received	Acknowledged
Four sent	Special train coming
Four received	Acknowledged

What happened in the 1907 accident was that the understanding of these bells was reversed. Each signalman thought he was asking for clearance and hence considered that he had been given the go-ahead, whereas the opposite was true.

The bells and bell pushes were located in small signal boxes, the south located some 40 to 50 yards from the tunnel entrance. The signal men were Dockyard labourers, permanently appointed to the task, and equally permanently stationed at each end, their hours of working being 6.20 a.m. to 5.30 p.m. with a half-hour lunch break. The bells were battery operated and not particularly loud. There was no telephone between the boxes. The south signal man also operated the hand-worked points immediately adjacent to his station, but the north one did not regularly do so. The instruction to proceed into the tunnel was by word of mouth from the signalman to the shunter, who accompanied each train, who would then tell the driver. This choice of word of mouth system is remarkable given the well known accident on the Cornwall Railway at Menheniot in 1873. On this occasion the signalman had called out 'Right-away, Dick' when two trains were in the station heading in opposite directions but both with drivers called Dick. The wrong train started off and a head-on collision resulted shortly after.

The recommendations of the Coroner's jury after the 1907 inquest were heeded by the Admiralty and a Webb & Thompson Miniature Electric Train Staff system was installed in about 1910. This was the product of the Railway Signalling Company of Liverpool and in this form was a new invention, having only been introduced in 1906, although the idea on a larger physical scale had been in use since 1888. The system basically required the driver of a train only to

A rare pair of Webb & Thompson Train Staff Apparatus, with consecutive serial numbers M607 & M608. These are the oldest known in existence and survive in the Plymouth Naval Base Museum.
P. BURKHALTER

83

Controlling the North Yard approach to the tunnel was a small cabin opposite the Dockyard Central Offices. This photograph dates from sometime in the 1950s. B MENNIE

proceed on a single line when he had possession of the train staff. This was a metal round bar, some 10 inches long, with collars on its length. The collars fitted slots in machines, which permitted the release of the staffs by electric means, and prevented (by locking) the opposite end machine from releasing a staff when one was already issued from the other end. This simple but effective idea was the invention of Messrs. Webb & Thompson of the London & North Western Railway. The Railway Signalling Co. installed instruments number M607 and M608 in the signal boxes at either end with a total of 20 staffs. These are the earliest known examples of these machines to survive and they have been preserved in the Plymouth Naval Base Museum. It is also rare for them to be consecutively numbered in the same connected site, as usually they were moved around after being away for repair.

Signal boxes, small ground level timber buildings with extensive glazing, were located in front of the south Smithery and at the foot of the road incline outside Central Offices, and these housed the Webb & Thompson instruments. The signal boxes also controlled colour light signals, installed by 1932, which indicated to both road and rail traffic at the north and south tunnel exits, whether the way was clear for either mode of transport. Due to the layout at the south end, the system here was extensive, extending as far south as the Joiners' Shop. As late as 1996 at least four of the signals survived in-situ, although not in use. Upon the construction of the Frigate Refit Complex in 1970 the north signal box was removed and the instrument housed across the road in the boiler room of Central Offices. At the other end, the box had to go when the road bridge between South and Morice Yard was constructed and then a small room immediately adjacent to the tunnel portal was used. The bell signals and operating instructions in connection with this system are given in Appendix One.

To allow access to the branches into Morice Yard (Gun Wharf) and to the Coal Yard, both of which were between the instruments, an arrangement attached to the point lever comprised a sliding tray into which the staff dropped, which then slid into the point lever base and unlocked the lever. This meant that the points could only be operated when the staff was out of the block instruments and could be placed in the sliding tray. Also at Morice Yard was a stop-block on the branch line, operated by rodding off the point lever, to stop any wagons being pushed onto the main line and fouling through movements. This was said to be rather stiff to pull over due to the length of rodding.

The railway was run by the Constructive Department, until a decision was made in 1932 to transfer responsibility to Superintending Naval Stores Officer (SNSO), re-named in January 1969 as Principal Stores & Transport Officer (Navy) (PSTO(N)). A storehouseman, Mr Jack Moore, was appointed to the position Storehouseman Rail Traffic Office. From then until 1993 this organisation ran the railway, providing all the staff and 'owning' the internal wagons, but not the locomotives, drivers or permanent way men.

Rail transport staff provided by the Naval Stores Department were 17 in North Yard and eight in South Yard. These included five and three for shunting, plus the signalmen and supervisory staff. The two guards for the passenger trains had separate detailed instructions, as did the flagmen. Two full-time signalmen were positioned north and south of the tunnel, the former also controlling movements northwards from that location. Three other flagmen were employed; one at the north end of the Narrows (the roadway squeezed between the Quadrangle and the Keyham College wall), one at the junction into the Exchange Sidings and one to the north of this latter location adjacent to the North Dock Pumping Station.

The flagman would signal the trains through and stop traffic approaching a train heading in the opposite direction. They worked out of cabins which were connected by telephone, although the system was not entirely foolproof as reversals back along the line were not uncommon.

We have been fortunate in that the detailed railway operating instructions for 1933 have survived, and a précis follows. It can be assumed that, like the main line sectional appendices, these did not change much over the years so were probably those initiated after the tunnel accident in 1907.

> Road traffic to the tunnel vaults was protected by a signal and a bell which was rung by the North Yard signalman each time he sent a train through.
>
> A detailed record of truck movements, both external and internal, was kept, and a strict record of their usage maintained, especially when transferred between Yards. It was permitted for goods trucks to be attached to the passenger train if urgently required.
>
> The signalmen were to count the number of trucks on each train passing into the tunnel and telephone this to their opposite number, to ensure that the train arrived complete.
>
> In the Principal Officers' carriage a First Aid box was carried.
>
> In the hours of darkness a red light was to be carried on the rear passenger coach and a white light was to be carried at the front of all locomotives.
>
> Very strict control is detailed in connection with handling of the main line wagons. Demurrage was to be avoided at all costs.
>
> Accidents were classified into two categories, involving personal injury or otherwise. The former were treated very seriously with a Board of Inquiry being formed of Senior Officers of the Dockyard. Minor incidents could be dealt with at a more junior level.

The single line section from Keyham Junction to the Exchange Sidings is controlled by this Staff. P. BURKHALTER

Locomotives had to be kept fully employed. The complement in 1933 was defined as two for passenger work, and eight for goods (though there were more locomotives at that time).

So as not to unduly disturb important meetings being held in the Board Room of the Central Offices, all guards were to make sure unloading noise was to be minimised, and drivers were directed to use their whistles as little a possible.

All trucks were to be checked under the loading gauge before being sent into the tunnel and the shunters were to be provided with lamps for poor visibility work. The shunters' minimum age was set at 18.

Precautions were laid down for workmen undertaking repairs in the tunnel, with a lookout being provided. The operating hours for the railway were from 6.30 a.m., to 5.30 p.m. Monday to Thursday, 5 p.m. on Friday, and 12.30 p.m. on Saturday.

As a result of a fatality in the early 1930s, when a workman fell off while attempting to ride on a passenger train by standing on the running board of a coach, the rules of such services were tightened. Any offenders were to be reported and disciplinary action would follow.

Rules still in existence in the 1968 'Instructions for locomotive drivers shunters & flagmen' (reprinted 1972) included the instruction to drivers 'Do not leave your steam engine unattended' but this rather out of date note had been removed by the 1978 edition of this booklet. This latter version carried the photograph of a Barclay side coupled diesel on the cover. These pocketbooks were issued by Ministry of Defence Dockyards organisation for use in all the establishments.

Responsibility for the railway operation passed from PSTO(N) to the new Dockyard management company, Devonport Management Ltd., on 4 October 1993. A new rule book, to fully reflect the current operating conditions and modern practice, was introduced on 4 January 1994 to coincide with the commencement of the HST coach project referred to earlier.

CHAPTER ELEVEN
MAIN LINE SERVICES

It must be said from the outset that, despite the provision of a platform at the Barracks and the very large number of workers who would have travelled to work in the Dockyard, there has never been a direct scheduled passenger service from the main line. As early as July 1889, immediately upon the Barracks being occupied, it had been suggested that a service from the Barracks Platform to Millbay would be of use, but this was not to be. We will see later that service specials were commonplace, but for the bulk of the Dockyard railway's life the mainstay has been freight.

FREIGHT SERVICES

It would seem that early services to the Dockyard, as indeed many local freight trains, did not appear in the Working Timetables. Whilst the branch opened in June 1867, no word of a scheduled service appeared until the first years of this century. The somewhat sparse service down the main line may well not have needed a defined 'path' for the freight needs of the Yards. However, it can be surmised that as a result of the large increase in GWR suburban services in the Plymouth area, brought about by the decision to

30216 on the connecting line from the Southern to the Western at St. Budeaux with the Dockyard Goods on 10 April 1952. A LATHEY

0-6-0 PT 9711 propelling the Dockyard Transfer out onto the main-line on 23 April 1957, the signals indicating that the road has been set for the up main. A Dockyard Policeman observes the event. The circular object on the left is a wartime 'pill-box', which is still there in 1996.
A LATHEY

compete with the new electric trams and with the new L&SWR line into Plymouth, there was needed a more rigorous approach. In July 1904 a steam rail motor service was introduced between Saltash and Plympton which had over 34 trains each way on weekdays. From this time the pattern of trains for the next seventy years was set, with both companies providing a freight train or two into the Dockyard each weekday. The starting point of these services was, for the L&SWR, Devonport (Kings Road) and, for the GWR, the extensive yards at Laira and Tavistock Junction on the eastern approaches to the city.

The first mention in a Working Timetable was in January 1903 when the GWR showed a service conveying 'traffic for HM Dockyards' leaving Laira at 2.05 p.m., and returning with 'traffic from HM Dockyards' from Keyham at 4.10 p.m.

Appearing in the Winter 1905 schedules was the first mentioned L&SWR service to Keyham, which reversed at North Road at 11.45 a.m., arrived at Keyham 10 minutes later, then returned just under an hour later. At 1.45 p.m. the GWR left Laira Junction with a transfer freight hauled by the Yealmpton goods loco. This arrived at Keyham at 2.5 p.m. and remained here for 2 ½ hours before the return run. Whilst in 1924 the SR service was much the same, the Great Western had bought their's forward to 12.23 p.m. at Keyham, returning at 1.30 p.m. to Laira Junction Yard.

After the Second World War the Southern were still the first in the day, with a transfer into the Yard at around 10.05 a.m., leaving again at 10.30 a.m. This was after the wartime connection at St Budeaux had opened in 1941, allowing the running of the service from Devonport Kings Road via this route

Though published before, this 1956 view of 4858 shunting in the Sidings is worthy of inclusion for two reasons. Firstly for the BR(W) 0-6-0 PT of the 5700 class No 9711 and secondly for a glimpse of Dave Rogers in 4858, a Dockyard driver until his retirement in 1993.
HUGH DAVIES

The opposite extremes of diesel power in the Dockyard sidings in October 1992. Devonport Mangement Ltd. were using the chassis of this withdrawn class 47 loco, 47538, for use as an engine test bed. On the right are 4858 and 4860.
P. BURKHALTER

rather than via North Road. The GWR came later in the day with two services, one at approaching 1 p.m., the other about 4 p.m. Over the years the exact times varied slightly but the basic pattern remained the same.

Under British Railways in 1962 the service was provided by the Southern Region at 10.05 a.m. (as before), then the Western Region left Tavistock Junction at 10.20 a.m., visiting the Dockyard sidings twice, at 1.55 p.m. and 3.55 p.m., to clear traffic to Keyham before returning to Tavistock Junction Up Yard at 6.05 p.m. Once the Southern's Kings Road to St Budeaux section closed, the service remained, but now incorporated into the WR one, to give three visits a day; one from Kings Road, running via North Road to reverse, and the others from the eastern yards.

Generally all freight services were confined to Monday to Friday, although Saturday trains were provided for, but with a note that they were suspended. Presumably the facility was there should the need arise. From time to time an early Monday freight worked to clear weekend traffic. On an as required basis some trips extended to Bullpoint RN Depot, served by a short branch at the north end of Weston Mill Viaduct, it being convenient to service this from Keyham.

The Dockyard locomotive would very often bank the main line freight up the hill to Keyham, or collect wagons left on the branch at Keyham, which practices lasted until the early 1980s.

The Great Western, and later BR, had a foreman or porter stationed in the Railway Office at the sidings to handle the liaison between the Yard and themselves for incoming and outgoing freight.

MAIN LINE LOCOMOTIVES

At the time of the opening of the connection at Keyham in 1867, the locomotives to be seen on freight turns to the Yard were probably of the fourteen broad gauge 0-6-0 saddle tanks of either Great Western origin or purchased from the Avonside Engine Co. (and predecessors) that operated the SDR and Cornwall Railway in the area. Later acquisitions were built as convertibles (that is, being convertible from broad to standard gauge) but were still 0-6-0 goods engines. At the turn of the century the 1854 and 2721 classes, and later the 57XX pannier tank class, worked the branch. Of the former two classes there were three at Laira and five at Millbay in 1902. In 1938 four 0-6-0 pannier tanks were based at Laira but this

After delivering freight into the exchange sidings, Laira based D7575 (later 25225) waits with only the brake van for the branch signal to clear, to return to Tavistock Junction Yard, on 28 March 1972.
ALISTAIR JEFFERY

On 22 June 1992, 37670, usually seen on china clay trains, delivers five VGA vans for trials with RNAD Ernesettle's Unimog road/rail tractor. As there had been no movements over the branch since relaying in March 1992 close interest was paid to progress. In the background is Drake Platform. P. BURKHALTER

number had increased to 19 immediately after the end of the War. 9711 was recorded at various dates between 1938 and 1959 on turns into the Yard and was regularly seen until leaving Laira in 1961. Also 63XX and 78XX types were seen here on occasions, although the latter were not popular due to difficulties with their vacuum brakes. The only engines banned from the branch were the 47XX and 60XX (King) classes, very large locomotives indeed.

During the war a solitary 0395 class was shedded by the Southern at Friary and would be seen on transfer freights, the only tender engine ever on this duty. In the 1960s the Southern goods could be hauled by an E1R, N, 02, M7 or LMS 2-6-2T. Later, BR standard diesels such as Hymek and D600 classes, plus the inevitable 08 shunter, would be seen. Other recorded BR locomotives on the branch were from classes 25, 31, 37 and 47. A rare visit by a class 50 occurred on 25 September 1986, when 50006 *Neptune* conducted a clearance test on the branch. This was preparatory to the proposed cresting of sister engine 50032 *Courageous* by the crew of the Royal Navy submarine of the same name at the platform in HMS Drake.

MAIN-LINE PASSENGER SPECIALS

The provision of passenger trains has always been for Navy personnel only but, due to their nature, were arranged at short notice and, according to one signalman, the daily notice announcing the special usually arrived days after the train had actually run. A very early published reference, in the *Naval &*

Military Record of 18 July 1889, that is, immediately after the opening of the Barracks, mentions the running of experimental trains in the previous few days. This report goes on to repeat rumours that the forthcoming fleet review in the Spithead would see such trains in use for troop movements. It is clear from this report that such trains had not been previously run, so we have a potential date for the introduction of such services.

The sparse data that does exist shows some spectacular trains. In December 1944 a 12 coach special started from Admiralty Platform (as the Barracks Platform was also known), being hauled onto the main line by two pannier tanks, then a King class and a Bulldog class backed from Keyham onto the train, before setting off towards North Road. Another recorded instance was on 13 December 1953 when a 14 coach leave special, for Birmingham Snow Hill, left the Platform in the Barracks double-headed, running via the SR connection at St Budeaux. Many services ran onto and off the branch for major cities around the country either immediately before or after holiday periods, or at other times to move ships' complements from base to base. These trains could be formed entirely of other railway companies' stock. One long-serving Navy officer recalls a lengthy journey from Rosyth to Devonport, dispatched with a packed meal for the 16 hour journey. These trains started from all over the Yard, from the dockside next to the ship, or from the track inside St Levans Gate, picking up the officers at Admiralty Platform.

Four rare visits by enthusiast railtours occurred, all organised by the Branch Line Society. The first was on Saturday 10 October 1970, when a three car suburban diesel multiple unit travelled the freight lines of Plymouth, plus the Gunnislake branch. At about 5 p.m. on that day, by special arrangement with the Dockyard authorities, it travelled down to the Exchange Sidings, with 84 passengers on board. To accord with a photographic ban all the cameras on board were locked in a spare compartment for the duration of the passage of Navy property.

The second of these events was on Saturday 10 May 1980 when a tour of the South Devon freight branches ran from Bristol. Once again a late afternoon visit to the Exchange Sidings was possible, and enjoyed by 159 passengers.

The Branch Line Society organised another visit on 14 October 1981, when 20 members arrived by road to be conveyed around the system from North Yard through the tunnel to South Yard, in open wagons hauled by Planet loco Yard No 5200. The visitors were advised that much of the railway had not been traversed for six months or more, so indicating the run-down before cessation of rail service. Once again the BLS paid a visit during a railtour on Saturday 11 March 1995. A fully loaded class 150, 150248, arrived at Keyham at 11.14 from Bristol and travelled down the branch to the Exchange Sidings. A shuttle to and from Admiralty Platform was performed and the train left at just before 1 p.m. en-route to Par Harbour, before returning to Bristol.

On Saturday 30 March 1985 a student training special arrived at 5 a.m. in support of a military exercise, the last recorded occasion

A unique photograph of a Navy special in November 1971 at Admiralty Platform. Note the timber platform extension that was later removed. That apart, and a new concrete retaining wall to the right, the scene is little changed today, and visible from the public road. B MILLS

The Navy special reversing out onto the down main line at Keyham in November 1971. The mechanical signalling here only lasted until 2 July 1973. A loaded bogie truck has been left on the loop by BR, and is waiting for the Dockyard loco to collect it. Note that since the April 1957 photograph on page 88, the starting signal has been repositioned to provide better visibility. B MILLS

of a loaded passenger working for the Navy.

The reason for opening Keyham station on 1 July 1900 has been described elsewhere. Specific services have been run to terminate at this point, rather than the principal stations of Plymouth, just for the Navy. Some post-war examples are for Navy Days. On 1 August 1949 a seven coach Castle class locomotive-hauled special left Penzance at 11.15 a.m. calling at most intermediate stations to Keyham, arriving there at 1.55 p.m. It then formed the North Road to Liverpool service.

In the last decade before the Second World War, the Sunday overnight train from Paddington stopped only to put off passengers at Keyham at 4.30am. The rail motor services, to and from Saltash, were heavily used by Dockyard workers, to the extent that the GWR working timetables had specific references to amendments required to suit the Dockyard employees' working arrangements, such as additional Yard holidays when the services would not have been necessary.

Leave specials at holiday times were a feature. On Friday 19 December 1952 there was a departure from the Keyham up loop platform at 10.5 a.m. (the empty stock working having left Millbay at 9.20 a.m.) for Bristol Temple Meads without stopping at North Road, to carry 60 sailors for south Wales, 113 for the London Midland Region and 151 for the following Penzance to Crewe service.

In the Summer 1993 schedules, which were repeated that winter, was an unusual working leaving Portsmouth Harbour on Sunday night at 10.28 p.m., and running via Salisbury and Westbury to terminate at Keyham at 2.44 a.m. The train then ran empty to either Saltash or St Budeaux Victoria Road where it could reverse, the movement being controlled from the Panel Box at Plymouth.

Over a period of 25 years the Branch Line Society has visited the Dockyard Branch with rail-tours. The third was on 11 March 1995, when Regional Railways two-car DMU 150248 is seen in the sidings. P. BURKHALTER

CHAPTER TWELVE
PERMANENT WAY

The earliest surviving details of track construction date from 1887, and describe new track in Devonport Yard having a concrete foundation with longitudinal timber baulks upon which were laid 68 lb (per yard) bridge rail spiked down. Between the rails, granite setts were laid level with the track, except to both rails where chequer plate fixed to timber blocks provided the groove for the flange.

The specification for the Extension Works in 1896 called for flat bottom rails of 75 lb weight fixed to the sleepers with wood screws and clips to standard gauge. Crossings and switches were held in chairs, and constructed of the same weight rail. 4,700 yards of track were laid of which 1,000 yards were curved. There were nine sets of ordinary turnouts and one diamond crossing.

In 1955 most of the trackwork in the Dockyard was 75 lb and 95 lb flat bottom rail spiked directly to sleepers. Short sections of dock rail of 126 lb weight could be seen to the north of the tunnel (180 yards) and south of the South Yard Mould Shop (80 yards), and 800 yards of bullhead rail was still laid in South Yard. Where the tracks met the roadways it was set into cobbles, or concrete road. Some concrete sleepers were laid in the tunnel in 1942, presumably to counter the very wet conditions experienced. Elsewhere timber sleepers were in use. Extracted below is a schedule from 1955 recording the length of trackwork. What is remarkable is the total number of turnouts and crossings, 414 or an average of one every 100 yards of track.

Generally the condition was deplorable, with rotten timber sleepers or broken concrete ones. Broken rails, sunken roads and

Devonport - H. M. Dockyard Permanent Way.
Standard Gauge January 1955

Location	Crossings		Length of Track		Totals	
	Common	Diamond	In the Open	Inside Buildings		
	Number	Number	Yards	Yards	Yards	Miles
Line from BR to sidings	2	-	1,070	-	1,070	0.61
Reception Sidings	6	-	1,220	-	1,220	0.69
North Yard	216	28	24,220	1,170	25,390	14.43
South Yard	132	25	10,880	430	11,310	6.43
Morice Yard	3	-	570	-	570	0.32
Tunnel	2	-	1,000	-	1,000	0.57
Totals	**361**	**53**	**38,960**	**1,600**	**40,560**	**23.05**

roller coaster trackwork were all in evidence. Certainly after this date substantial remedial works were put in hand and eventually all the rail was converted to dock rail, except for some remote locations in South Yard. As part of this improvement work rail joints were made using the Thermit process of welding, the first time that this had been undertaken in the Yard.

Steady development over the years is evident from the regular entries in the Annual Navy Estimates placed before Parliament. (See Appendix Two) Drawings survive from Edgar Allen & Co. Ltd. of Sheffield, manufacturers of rail turnout materials, with new rail layouts east of No 5 and No 6 Docks in 1966, north east corner of No 4 basin in 1967 and a new siding for a transit shed to the east of the Exchange Sidings (the rail was laid but the shed not built) as recently as 1984.

After the cessation of rail usage of the tunnel the Dockyard Authorities moved to disconnect the railway where no longer needed. In 1984 the opportunity was taken to reconstruct the road through the Narrows (the road running to the east of the Quadrangle up against the retaining wall) and as a result the railway south of St Levans Gate to the tunnel approach was removed. In all 300 metres of rail track was lifted in this particular operation. At later stages other areas were removed, such as to the east of No 3 basin in 1988, and on No 6 wharf in 1994.

During the first three months of 1992 the section of track passing through HMS Drake received a major upgrading, carried out for Devonport Management Limited by the railway engineering contractors, Grant Lyon Eagre Ltd. The headshunt at Keyham Junction was taken out and the turnout removed, and many sleepers also were renewed.

TURNTABLES

As may be expected in such confined locations in and around the buildings and docks of the Yard, there was widespread use of wagon turntables. Surprisingly the greater number were located in North Yard, whereas it could have been anticipated that the older, more crowded confines of South Yard would have created the need for such items. In the event only two turntables appear to have been installed in South Yard, two in Morice Yard and 18 in total in North Yard, although not all at the same time.

The earliest indicated on the plans was on the west side of the Quadrangle to give access to the centre door into the building and then across the courtyard central area. This one is shown on the plan accompanying the Cornwall Railway agreement of December 1865 as already in existence. The advent of the main line broad gauge connection saw the installation of two 44 feet diameter tables, one at the foot of the 1 in 70 gradient at the very north end of the Yard (as it existed then) which allowed the transfer of rolling stock onto the east-west line on the northern side of the Quadrangle. At the end of this track there was another 44 feet table to access the lines on the east wharf of No 3 basin. No constructional details survive of these two large turntables, but it can be surmised that due to their size they were open, that is, not decked in. These two lasted for the remainder of the century, with the north-eastern one being the subject of correspondence in the First World War. Internal memoranda between the Civil Engineer and the Engineering Department deal with the operational problems should the turntable be removed, and the figure of £930 was quoted to lay in the replacement trackwork curves to enable six-wheel trucks to reach the basin-sides. There the matter rested until December 1915 when the Divisional Superintendent of the GWR wrote to the Admiral Superintendent to state that difficulties were experienced operating Troop trains into the Yard as the GWR locomotives were not permitted to pass across this turntable. The GWR went on to ask if permission could be given to remove this restriction as it would allow 'economy of engine power and time'. After examining diagrams of the 2-6-2T and 4-4-0 Bulldog classes the directive was issued that only the tank locomotive was to pass over this table, and then only if the attached trucks

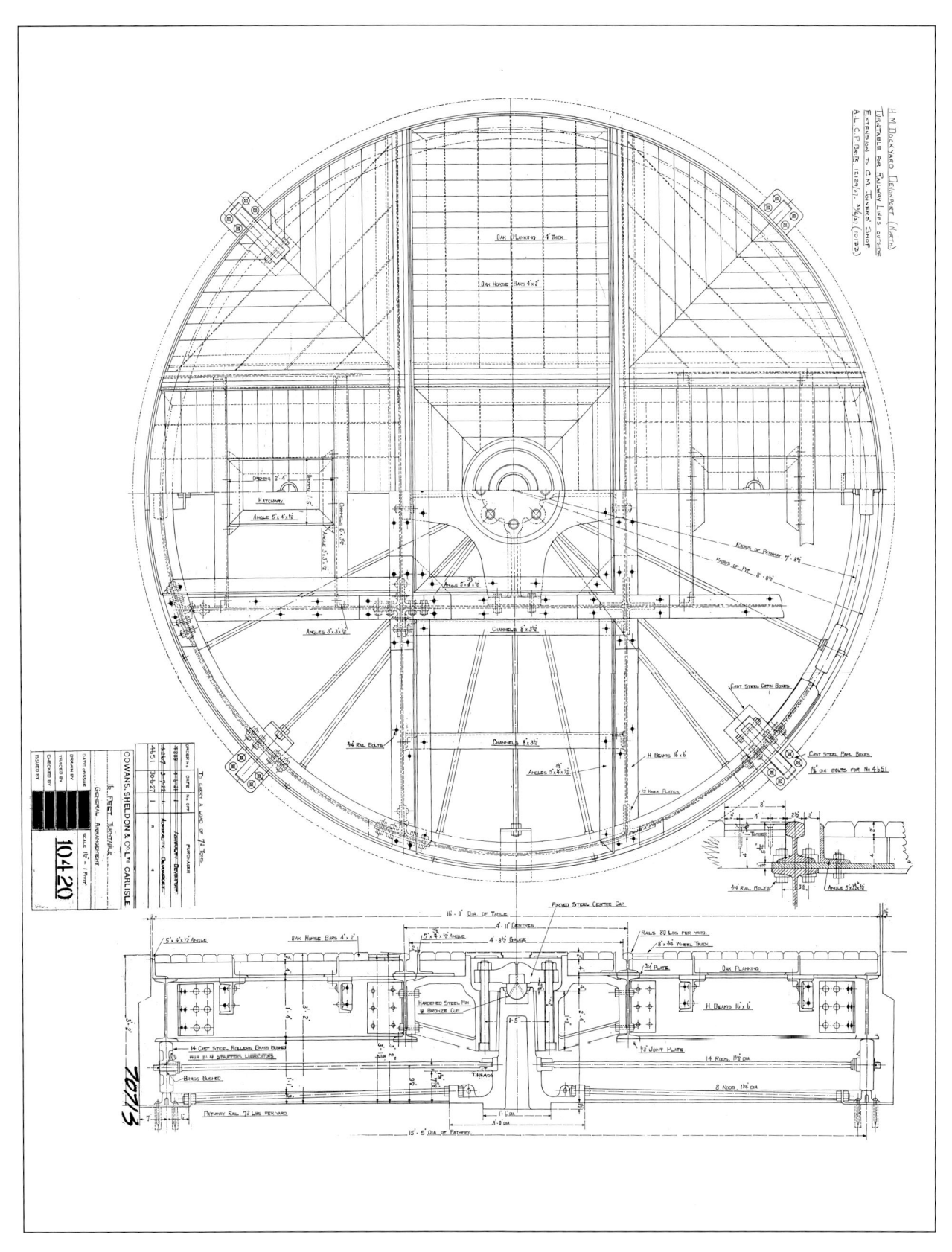

Details of the turntables installed in the 1920s outside the Joiners Shop and the Torpedo Shop in North Yard

or carriage would not exceed a total of 65 tons. It would seem that the solution of new trackwork was more convenient as some time later in 1916 the turntable was removed.

The drawings show that these two large turntables, plus two of the standard 16 feet tables, were provided with mixed gauge tracks. One of these smaller ones from the east side of No 3 basin ended up in South Yard, where it has remained since, only being discovered for what it was in 1992. The standard gauge tracks only exist in one direction, with the broad gauge in both. In August 1996, this was removed from its location to avoid damage, for preservation at the Plymouth Naval Base Museum.

Various other tables were supplied in the later years of the nineteenth century, then a number were installed in the new Extension works, completed in 1906. None appear in Jackson's contract so it would seem that the Admiralty decided to purchase and install them themselves.

Cowans & Sheldon of Carlisle won the majority of the tenders for the supply, for the same design. The specification for Yard No 7 can be quoted from, in summary, to indicate the general type:

A steel centre pin and cup arrangement provided a spindle for the table to rotate upon. The maximum working load was 72 tons, but a test of 108 tons was to be applied by a 8 wheel bogie truck being run onto the turntable. The main girders, located under the rails were 16in x 6in rolled steel joists. The peripheral load would be carried by a ring of 14 disc rollers running on a circular track, with axles reaching to the centre post. The rails were to be 80lb BS flat bottom, and these were set flush in a deck of English Oak finished with two coats of tar. To hold the table in position, steel pawls dropped into boxes set into the granite outer ring. There was to be central casting carrying the name of the manufacturer, the year and the Yard number, with working and test loads stated.

The last table to be supplied was in 1957. This was unique because if the standard size of 16 feet had been supplied, then one rail of the 25 feet gauge crane track running along the dockside, where the turntable was to be located, would have had to be incorporated. This was deemed rather impractical, so the diameter was reduced to 12 feet. Advances of technology had not impressed themselves upon the Dockyard, as the manufacturer had to gently suggest some modern expanding bolt fixings, in place of distinctly antiquated methods specified.

When the railway ceased internal freight by rail in 1982 all the turntables fell into disuse and were mostly broken up for scrap. The very last two in North Yard survived in position until 1993, although neither was in use. One from the rear of the North Yard workshop, which also served the Joiner's Shop in earlier years, has been sold into preservation at a private railway at Bere Ferrers. The other was removed from its site south of the Exchange Sidings early in 1994 and stored until acquired by the Shackerstone Railway and removed in November 1995

CHAPTER THIRTEEN
THE LOCOMOTIVES

Some seventy locomotives are recorded as having been in the Dockyard in the 130 years or so since the small, odd-looking Aveling & Porter first steamed in the mid-1860s. One common factor applies to almost every one, in that they only had two axles (the exceptions were six in Jackson's fleet). The very tight curves of the Dockyard tracks have always ruled out anything of three axles being practicable. It should also be noted that all the Devonport locomotives were standard (4 feet 8½ in) gauge, or less.

This chapter will deal in depth with all the locomotives, by builder works number, identifying the Admiralty engines and those of the contractors. All the engines also appear in tabular form showing principal dimensions.

Whilst most of the Admiralty locomotives saw out their entire lives at this location, the contractors' engines travelled to construction sites far and wide, often unrecorded. Therefore the details in this category are necessarily not intended to be exhaustive.

The Engineering Department 'owned' the locomotives, and they carried this department's name on the tanks until the 1960s. Until this time the livery of the locomotive fleet was plum lined in yellow, though dull red may be a more appropriate description. The only exception was the new No 2 which was faded green lined in yellow. By 1976 the diesel locomotives were in a livery of dark green with the front and rear buffer beams diagonally striped in black and yellow.

There were two locomotive sheds, one each in North and South Yards. The South Yard shed was located immediately in front of the Smithery; indeed it was a lean-to arrangement attached to this building. Constructed of galvanised sheets on a heavy timber frame, the roof was very high to accommodate steam cranes also but with the jibs projecting. It lasted until the road fly-over was constructed in 1962. The North Yard shed was located outside the front of the Central Offices, and approached from the west. Built of masonry at the rear, and sheeting at the front, it could hold eight locomotives on three roads. Pits at the rear enabled repairs to be undertaken, although any heavy work would require the engine to be moved into one of the workshops in the Quadrangle. It was swept away in the preparations for construction of the covered dock Frigate Refit Complex in the 1970s.

At the end of the Second World War, the shed was staffed with one fitter, one boilermaker and a couple of labourers. An apprentice who worked here for a short period, Mr Jack Andrews, recalled 53 years later that a fitter working on a locomotive accidentally drove it through the back wall of the shed into the road outside.

AVELING & PORTER

In alphabetical order, A&P comes first, so it is fitting that this manufacturer was the first supplier to the Admiralty at Devonport. Thomas Aveling set up a small works in Rochester (Kent) in 1850 to repair agricultural machinery and the company soon became well-known for road traction engines, some of which were converted for rail use.

143: Between 1865 and 1867 a contractor, William Jackson, was working within the Dockyard on extensions to the North Basin (now No 3 basin). For some contractual reason, not readily explainable now, the Admiralty ordered for him a 10hp A&P standard design, works no 143. It was

The Aveling & Porter range of railway locomotives showed every sign of their traction engine heritage. Here is a contemporary at Chatham Dockyard in 1872. PUBLIC RECORD OFFICE ADM195/7

shipped out of Rochester on 15 May 1865, and was still with Jackson later that year as he wrote from Keyham Dockyard, Devonport on 6 November:

> Dear Sir,
> In reply to yours of the 1st inst., as to my opinion of the 10hp locomotive you have supplied to me for these works. I cannot speak too highly of it. I have been working it every day for four months on temporary roads, on rails varying from 36lbs to 42 lbs per yard. It will draw as many as 25 3 yard wagons loaded with slate stone rock, up an incline of 1 in 100 with perfect ease and having very little working gear, it is in as good order now as on the day it commenced work. It burns about 5cwt of coals per day and for slow work and economy has the advantage in every way over any other description of locomotive.
> Yours etc.

It is not at all certain what happened to this engine after completion of the works, whether it stayed with the Admiralty at Keyham or moved on with Jackson. In 1870 the trade press was carrying an advertisement for W. Jackson for the sale of two locomotives on completion of the Exmouth Docks & Railway, but nothing survives to identify them as being connected with the engine at Keyham.

An article in *Engineering* for 3 August 1866 extolled the virtues of A&P locomotives and was obviously an advertising exercise. Amongst many of the customers mentioned was the Admiralty. Other than works number 143 mentioned above, there were three more locomotives built for the Admiralty. They were works no 129 (8hp), ex works on 21 January 1865; 182 (6hp), ex works 4 April 1866; and 218 (8hp), ex works 3 August 1866. Part of what *Engineering* said was:

> Messrs Aveling & Porter have made two for the Royal Dockyards at Chatham and Devonport, as well as one for Portsmouth, now in hand. At Devonport the engine (which is of 10HP) has been working regularly on rails weighing from 36 to 42lb per yard, its daily consumption being about 5cwt of coals.

Note that the wording used exactly matches that of Jackson's letter. As no 218 was only out-shopped on the same date as the article in *Engineering*, it can be concluded that this was the Portsmouth one. Of the other two, neither is of the power quoted in

Engineering (10hp), so the conclusion is that the writer of the *Engineering* piece had forgotten the one sold to Jackson.

450: One other A&P was definitely at Devonport, being works number 450, sent away on 13 March 1869 for the Admiralty. Once again no later history of this engine has survived.

As can be seen from the photographs of similar engines, Aveling's designs owed much to the origins of the company, being visibly a road traction engine adapted for rails. The wheels were solid discs, chain driven to both axles from a flywheel balanced drive shaft mounted over the boiler, itself driven by a single cylinder. No connecting rods were therefore necessary.

Of these old A&P types, one is preserved, the slightly later 1872-built works no 807, which survives as a static exhibit at the London Transport Museum in Covent Garden.

The remaining reference, that can be deduced to refer to the Avelings, is nearly 30 years on, when the newspaper *Railway & Shipping Contractor* of 19 January 1893 included this editorial item:

> A new locomotive is shortly to be supplied to Devonport Dockyard in place of the old-fashioned engine which has drawn the Dockyard train for so many years. It has been found that the gradient between Keyham and the Naval Barracks is somewhat too steep for the present locomotive when required to draw a heavy load, but anyone could have seen that long ago.

The language would infer only one engine, so perhaps as Jackson was genuinely pleased with his locomotive he did take it with him to Exmouth.

AVONSIDE

A sole example from this West Country builder, which perhaps is rather strange, they being one of the nearest large locomotive suppliers.

1690: This was a class SS1 of their standard range of designs, works order 2564, and allocated Yard No 12. It was ordered on 22 March 1915 by the Admiralty for direct delivery to Devonport. The Yard number was carried on a circular plate supplied at works.

Many drivers in the 1950s considered this to be the best or strongest of the locomotives at that time. It saw service principally in North Yard and Extension Yard, until withdrawal from active service about July

No 12 in fine condition in 1951 under the coal loading gantry at the northern end of North Yard, also known as Extension.
HAROLD D BOWTELL

A home made protection for the footplate crew on No 12, here seen on the approach line to the North Yard shed in the 1950s.
B MENNIE

1956. However this was not the final demise of 1690 as, like so many of the others, it was pressed into use as a stationary boiler until final scrapping in 1959.

W. G. BAGNALL Ltd.

2962: The post-war market obviously was buoyant enough to justify building for stock, as on 19 January 1948 number 2962 was ordered on the works without any buyer in mind. In fact it was not until the Admiralty Chatham order dated 10 October 1949 arrived that it had an owner. On 12 July 1950 it left Bagnall's works at Stafford for Devonport. Construction was to standard E2665 drawings and it was to be supplied in plum livery, lined yellow and black with H. M. DOCKYARD DEVONPORT painted on each tank side. The number 19 was carried on a large rectangular plate. There is a story that on its first day of use in the Yard it de-railed a truck which resulted in the truck's buffers coming through the back sheet of the cab.

It turned out to be the last steam locomotive to be delivered to Devonport for by 1956 the diesels had arrived and from then on it was in use less and less. By early 1965 it had fallen out of regular operations, only 15 years old. With such little wear it also was put to use producing steam for the many needs of Dockyard operations, and could be seen at the head of No 8 dock until the late 1960s.

The Dockyard authorities then offered all the remaining steam locomotives for sale and No 19 became the property of the Cornwall Steam Locomotive Preservation Society. On 26 February 1969 one of the diesel Planets

No 19 in almost original condition in September 1951.
HAROLD D BOWTELL

towed the engine from its resting place by St Levan's Gate through the tunnel to South Slip where the large crane lifted it onto a lorry. It travelled into Cornwall via the Tamar Bridge, reputedly the first railway engine to have traversed the road bridge, its destination being the Great Western Society's depot at Bodmin General Station. Here restoration commenced, boosted in April 1969 when the plates, which had been destined for the Dockyard Museum, were officially presented to the new owners by the Dockyard Secretary, Mr Norman Chaff.

In 1977 all the stock at Bodmin was moved to the Imperial Kiln site at Bugle, which enjoyed rail access from the Goonbarrow China Clay branch. Shortly after this the lengthy restoration was complete and No 19 could return to active service by giving brake van rides. This role continued until 1986 when a return to Bodmin, now under the jurisdiction of the new Bodmin & Wenford Railway, was arranged on a trial period. So successful did this turn out that the arrangement became permanent the following year.

No 19 remains the only active steam locomotive surviving from Devonport (but see also Barclay 2221) and can be seen at Bodmin. In the days when operation was only within the station confines at Bodmin General No 19 was the stalwart, but since opening to Bodmin Parkway in 1990 the rather heavy gradient is more than she can handle so she is kept as a back-up and for special events. At Easter 1992 the South Devon Railway urgently needed some motive power and No 19 was loaned for a three week spell, which she discharged with honour.

At the back of the North Yard loco shed stands No 19 on 24 June 1965, 'ready for steaming', though not for long as steam usage ceased about this time.
R HATELEY

101

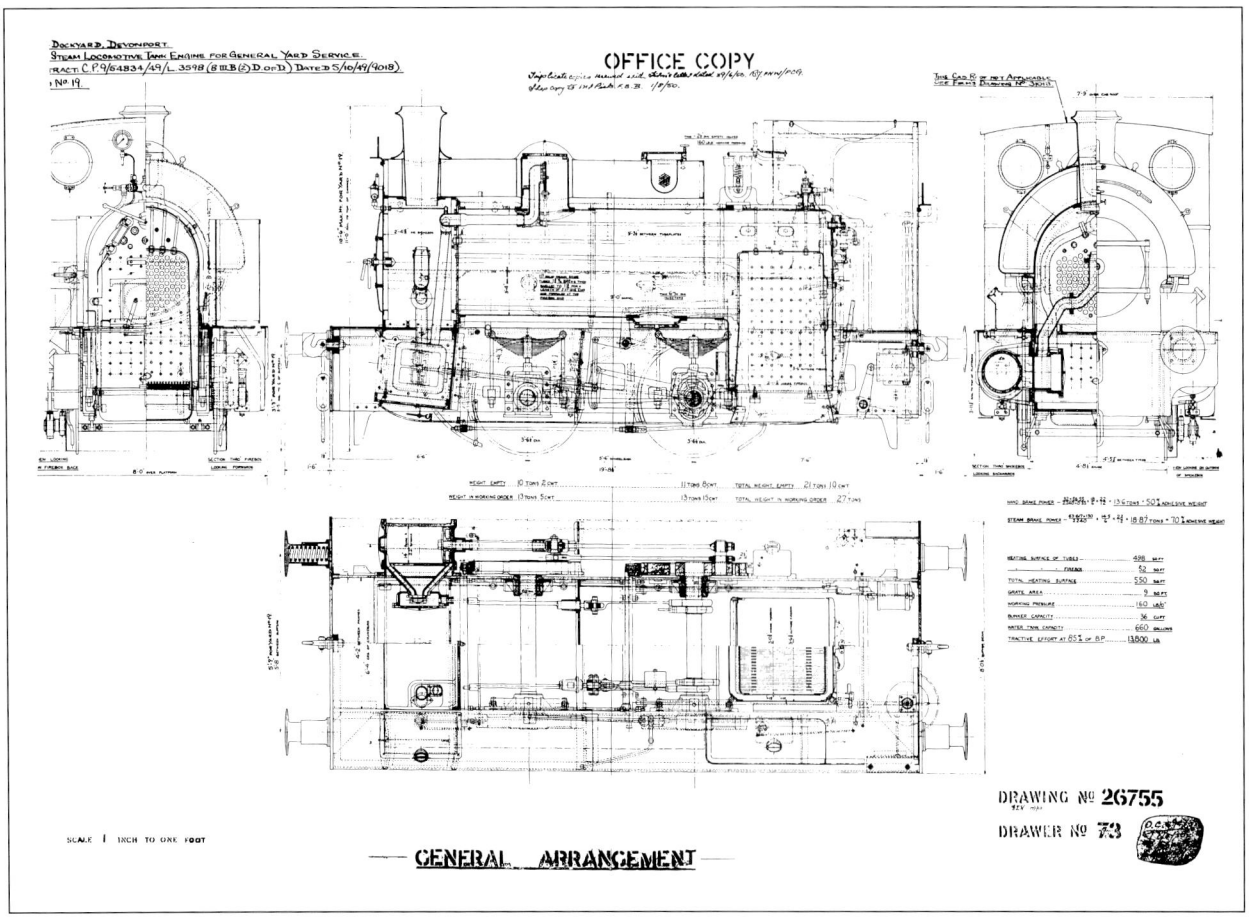

General arrangement of No 19

The original plates for No 19 are still carried, here captured while on shed at Bodmin in 1994. P. BURKHALTER

No 19 is in use at the Bodmin & Wenford Railway in Cornwall, though many regard the livery now carried as rather brighter than that seen in Dockyard days. Seen here at Bodmin Parkway on 28 June 1992. P. BURKHALTER

ANDREW BARCLAY & CO.

The Andrew Barclay engines had a distinctive style, as can be seen from the photographs, and were popular with all users. Those that saw service at Devonport came under both Sir John Jackson and the Admiralty.

BARCLAY LOCOMOTIVES OF SIR JOHN JACKSON

185: New to John Jackson on 30 May 1877 at his Stobcross Docks contract in Glasgow, where it appears to have acquired its name to match the city. Between 1886 and 1889 Jackson used it at North Sunderland harbour. Soon after contract commencement it was at work at Devonport, but then a gap appears until it turns up at the Heytesbury Military Railway (Wiltshire) in 1916, possibly as a requisitioned engine. After the end of the First World War it was stored at the War Office depot at Abbey Mills, London, from whence it appears to have been handed back to Jackson, for it was for sale by the firm in August 1921.

797: Again a new purchase by Jackson for the job in Fife at Burntisland Harbour, which opened in 1901. As was usual in such cases it acquired the name *Burntisland*, presumably by the workers on the next site who would refer to each loco by its previous location to identify it. At the end of contract auction sale conducted on 31 January 1907, it started off at £200, then rose in £10 and £5 bids until

This rather fuzzy enlargement of VICTORIA, Andrew Barclay works number 887, shows the Jackson plate above the builder's worksplate. V BRADLEY

Circumstantial evidence leads us to believe that Andrew Barclay works number 891 was with Jackson on the Extension Works at Keyham. Here photographed as late as 1 September 1962 still carrying the nameplates DOVER, at the John Knowles works in Derbyshire. R. HATELEY

South Yard had a huge loco shed as a lean-to structure to the smithery, the size of which also allowed the steam cranes to be shedded with their jibs still raised. Here No 10 stands rather lost in the early 1950s.
M DALY

reaching £350. Evidently this was less than the reserve, as it remained in Jackson's hands being sent overseas to either, or both, Vancouver and Singapore harbours. 797 crops up once more, as on 5 February 1929 the Barclay company received an order for spares to be shipped to Jackson via Alexandria for his contract to construct a barrage on the Upper Nile in Egypt. It is possible that this engine ended its days in the sun of North Africa.

810: Jackson got to the point of running out of his stock of locomotives for the huge new project at Keyham so he started ordering new. Barclay shipped this from Kilmarnock on 12 November 1897 with the name *Don Jose*. It obviously went about its business without any trouble as no spares were needed from the manufacturer. At the auction on 5 February 1907 at the completion of works it fetched £410, whereupon no more was ever heard of it.

853: Another of the new stock necessary for this undertaking. Sent from Barclay on 27 December 1899 direct to Keyham with the name *Ethel*. It performed without remark, and at the sale was knocked down for £580.

Once again it vanished from further record.

867: This engine was sent away from Kilmarnock to Jackson on 22 March 1900, without Barclay recording the delivery address. As Jackson was flat out at this time at Keyham it could be inferred that he had it here. It carried the name *Kathleen*.

887: Barclay records this as ex-works on 23 February 1901 with the name *Victoria* to Keyham. It evidently was returned to Jackson's Depot at Grays in Essex and passed over to Thomas W. Ward Ltd. when they acquired the Grays Yard in 1924, together with quite a lot of plant. Wards attempted to dispose of it, as it appears in a sale list in 1926, but apparently without success. It ended its days at Inverkeithing where Ward had a shipbreaking yard but spares were still being ordered for it in 1935.

891: Like 867 it left Kilmarnock without delivery location noted, on 10 December 1901. It carried the name *Dover* so may have gone to Jackson's job in Kent, but as the other locomotives ordered at this time were for Keyham it has been presumed to be here. Subsequently stored at the Grays depot it was sold by Wards to John Spencer Ltd. at Newburn Steelworks, Newcastle sometime between 1932 and 1943. Then via A. R. Adams, a dealer in Newport, to Pressed Steel Ltd., Cowley, Oxford. In 1949 the Ministry of Supply owned her until the following year, before passing to her final owner, John Knowles & Co. Ltd. of Woodville, Derbyshire, who scrapped her in 1967.

BARCLAY LOCOMOTIVES OF THE ADMIRALTY

1379 and **1380**: The first of the Kilmarnock output to come to Devonport for the Dockyard itself. Dispatched on 23 October 1914 and 3 November 1914 respectively, to an order from the Director of Navy Contracts on behalf of the Admiralty. Numbered 10 and 11 on oval plates, they wore the distinctive livery of red (or plum as it was officially known) with a brass band around the chimney, and carried large wooden buffer blocks rather than conventional sprung

THE LOCOMOTIVES

The crew pose for the photographer on 28 September 1951 in South Yard with No 11. Note the dumb buffers and bagged coal on the front buffer beam.
HAROLD D BOWTELL

A splendid view of No 13 arriving in South Yard on a passenger train on 25 May 1951. Note also the signalbox, and on the extreme left the large lean-to shed that could hold steam cranes; the jib of one can be seen. PLYMOUTH NAVAL BASE MUSEUM

105

The shunter with regulation pole strides along next to No 9 propelling wagons along the east side of 3 basin in about 1949. M DALY

A works photograph of No 16, delivered in 1919, with the legend of the Engineering Dept, as loco 'owners'

buffers. Certainly in later years they both stayed together in South Yard, but both appeared to be disused by March 1956. 1379 was withdrawn in August 1956 when it was broken up. 1380 was officially taken out of service in April 1957, but continued as a stationary boiler at the Transit Shed for a while after.

1397: Shortly after, and no doubt to further support the massive workload increase that the First World War had bought to the Yard, Andrew Barclay despatched this locomotive from the works on 12 April 1915 to the order of the Admiralty. Unlike the earlier twins, she had circular sprung buffers and was numbered 13. In post Second World War years this was the stalwart of the passenger service until being withdrawn from stock in January 1959, though apparently disused by September 1957.

1406: Yet another order for motive power in the early war years, but originally for Rosyth Dockyard, then relatively new. It travelled across Scotland on 25 March 1915 and entered service there as *Rosyth No 3*. An exact transfer date has not survived, but it was seen at Devonport on 9 October 1935, when it was carrying (somewhat eccentrically as it was out of numeric order) number 9. Withdrawal was about June 1956 and she was scrapped on site that year. Sister loco AB1385 also of 1914 and named *Rosyth No 1* has survived into preservation in the hands of the Railway Club of Wales, and is in working order on the Gwili Railway, Carmarthen.

1516: The last of the locomotives ordered at the time of the First World War, it was sent away from Kilmarnock on 8 April 1919, having had certain (unspecified) modifications made for the local requirements of Devonport, probably a cut down cab for the tunnel. Number 16 was allocated to it, and it worked mainly in North Yard until withdrawal and scrapping in November 1955.

2071: After a twenty year gap, the Navy returned to Andrew Barclay for No 17. Ordered by the Director of Navy Contracts on behalf of Devonport, it left Barclays on 2 October 1939. The detailed specification for this engine has survived, and in the four or so pages covers all the major components. Of particular interest is the inclusion of a spark cage, train vacuum brake, steel shutters to close off the cab openings, a livery in plum with ENGINEERING DEPARTMENT painted on either side of the cab. Principal dimensions were 23¾ tons in working order, working pressure of 150psi, 12 inch x 20 inch cylinders driving 3 feet 2 inch diameter wheels. A tale survives that a bomb fell near the loco during the Second War, slightly

THE LOCOMOTIVES

In the dying days of steam in 1963, No 17 shunts in the sidings. PLYMOUTH NAVAL BASE MUSEUM

General Arrangement of No 17

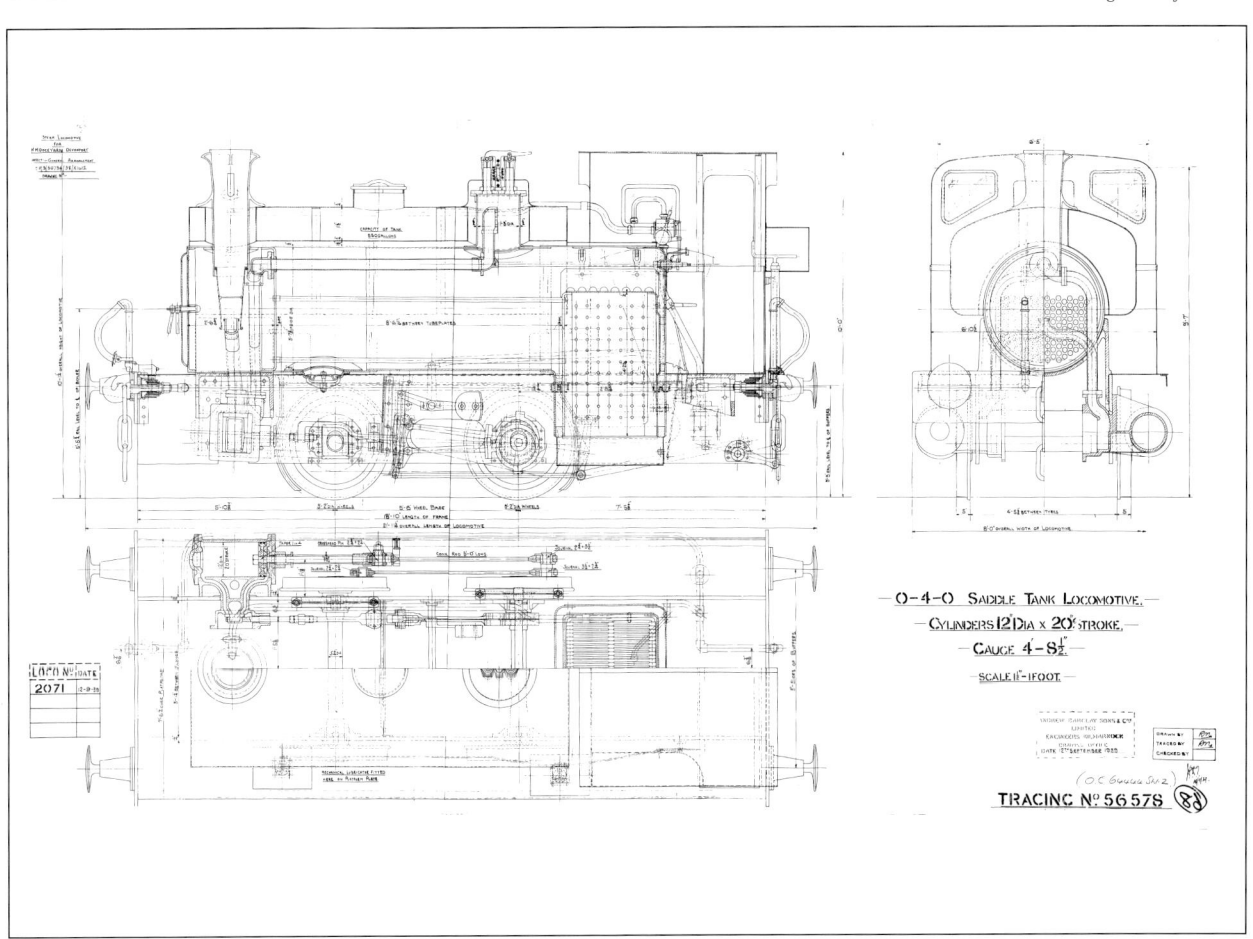

In the winter sunshine of January 1963, No 18 is shown off to visitors on the shed line in North Yard. P GRAY

twisting the chassis, a defect it carried for the rest of its days. A report of August 1961 has it just out of the workshops after a general overhaul, and being repainted in red with black boiler mountings. It seems to have worked right to the end of steam in May 1966 and then laid to one side until March 1968 when Hudsons of Dudley Ltd. purchased 17, 18 and 2. From there they passed it over to Small & Lewis of Gloucester who cut it up for scrap.

2137: In the Second World War additional engine power to supplement the ageing fleet was acquired. This locomotive was supplied on 12 March 1942, it was numbered 18. With only 20 years service it was mainly out of use by the early 1960s, although some repair work was done in 1961. One of the three locomotives purchased by Hudsons, it came to the same fate as No 17, this time in March 1968.

2221: The very last Barclay to come here, and the only one to have survived into preservation. Ordered by the Director of Contracts on 16 July 1945, it was dispatched on 16 October 1946. It (logically) carried No 19, but for some reason was later changed to 2, perhaps after the demise of the original 2 (HL2400), which number it carried on a small square plate. As supplied the cab was too high for the tunnel and only after alterations was it available for use through to South Yard. A story persists that, in fact, the loco was originally intended for Singapore Dockyard, and the cab roof was double skinned for added heat protection. Certainly it did not come with the usual plum livery, being painted in Olive Green and lined in yellow, hence popularly known as the 'Green Goddess'. For many years it was kept immaculate by an ex-Chief Petty Officer driver. 2221's principal claim to fame came on

No. 18 hauls the passenger on a rare occasion in March 1963. Here it is about to leave the northern terminus in North Yard. C Horsham

The worksplate of No 18
C Horsham

13 May 1966, when the last dockyard passenger train service ran. On that Friday, and the following Monday, Driver Alec Lambie was in charge of the flag-bedecked locomotive. After some time laid up out of sight behind the Turbine Shop, it went with 17 and 18 to Hudson's of Dudley, then onto a group of enthusiasts based at the Dowty Preservation Society in March 1968. It was steamed here in the early 1970s but restoration was required and this has proceeded slowly since. It moved to the Gloucester & Warwickshire Railway on 12 July 1983, then to its current location at the Dean Forest Railway (6 August 1988). The boiler has subsequently been away at Pridhams, ironically just up the Tamar estuary, at Gunnislake. In time it seems very likely that No 2 will be seen once again in steam. A success story on which to end this section.

BARCLAYS & Co.

Though bearing a similar name, and with very close business connections to Andrew Barclay & Son, Barclays & Co. were a separate company. The records relating to this company are sparse, so details are necessarily brief

229: Sir John Jackson acquired from an unconfirmed source works no 229 of 1876, which he named *Hamoaze*. At the end of contract sale it was disposed of at the knock down price of £225, which may have been merely the scrap value.

296: The other Barclays & Co. engine was not so publicity shy. Works number 296 was

No 2 (the second) carried every conceivable requirement on board! Here stood out of use on 24 June 1965. R Hateley

THE LOCOMOTIVES

In 1965 in the last few months before withdrawal, No 2 (the second) is seen shunting in the Exchange Sidings. C HORSHAM

built sometime in 1882 and somehow along the way acquired a plate reading 'Lennox Lange & Co. 1883'. This firm was a dealer, a mysterious operation with offices variously in London, Manchester and Glasgow, who had a habit of putting their plates on other builders' locomotives, causing no end of confusion.

However, maybe Jackson then bought 296 from them for his contract at Middlesbrough Docks (1882-1889), and that is where the name *Middlesbrough* came from. It came early in the Devonport contract, as Andrew Barclay supplied spares in February 1897 and again in May 1901. In the extensive workshops that

Driver Alec Lambie is on the footplate of No 2 waiting to leave South Yard on the last day of passenger services. The normal rules banning photography were passed over, as well as adherance to occupancy of the classes of accommodation on the train. PLYMOUTH NAVAL BASE MUSEUM

111

No 2 (Andrew Barclay works number 2221) survives, and is under long term restoration at the Forest of Dean Railway.
TERRY WALDRON

RIGHT: *Drewry works number 2177 nearly new in February 1946. This loco would see service in 15 military locations around Britain before arriving in Devonport carrying the Army number 249.* R TOURRET

Jackson had on site it received a major rebuild in 1903, which made it a sought after lot in the post-contract auction, the Admiralty paying £400 for it on 1 February 1907. On taking it into the Dockyard fleet it was given the number 3, though the name stuck. But disaster struck but a few months later, on the morning of Saturday 6 July 1907, when she crashed head-on into No 5 in the tunnel, wrecking the smaller loco and probably writing it off. No 3 returned under her own steam to the shed. After repairs she returned to an uneventful life. Sometime after October 1935 the Admiralty disposed of her to Wm. Gray & Co. Ltd., of West Hartlepool, where she carried the name *West Hartlepool No 2*. An unconfirmed sighting in 1964 had this engine derelict and about to be scrapped at Browney Colliery, without any identification, plates, etc.

THE DREWRY CAR COMPANY

Drewrys never actually built anything, as all the work was undertaken by other manufacturing concerns, and Drewry merely acted as a sales outlet.

A standard design was developed for the Ministry of Supply for a 150hp 0-4-0DM weighing 22½ tons and an order of twenty was fulfilled in 1941 which participated in the invasion of Europe, and in the Middle East. In 1945 another batch of twenty was ordered at a cost of £7,100 each, which Drewry farmed out to Vulcan (12) and Barclay (5). Events, however, had moved on and three of the orders were cancelled and never built. The remainder proved good workhorses for the various rail-connected army depots all over the British Isles, and some also saw service further afield.

In 1992 the decision was made to operate air-braked trains in the Dockyard. Various studies were carried out which put the option of upgrading the existing 'Planets' fairly low down the list, as the MOD found they had two of these Army Railway Organisation Drewrys spare. They lent themselves more readily to application of train air-braking systems, so these two came to Devonport. After arriving they have been repainted in a blue livery, with yellow and black striped ends.

2177 (Vulcan Works No 5258) has carried a variety of other numbers over the years. Its

THE LOCOMOTIVES

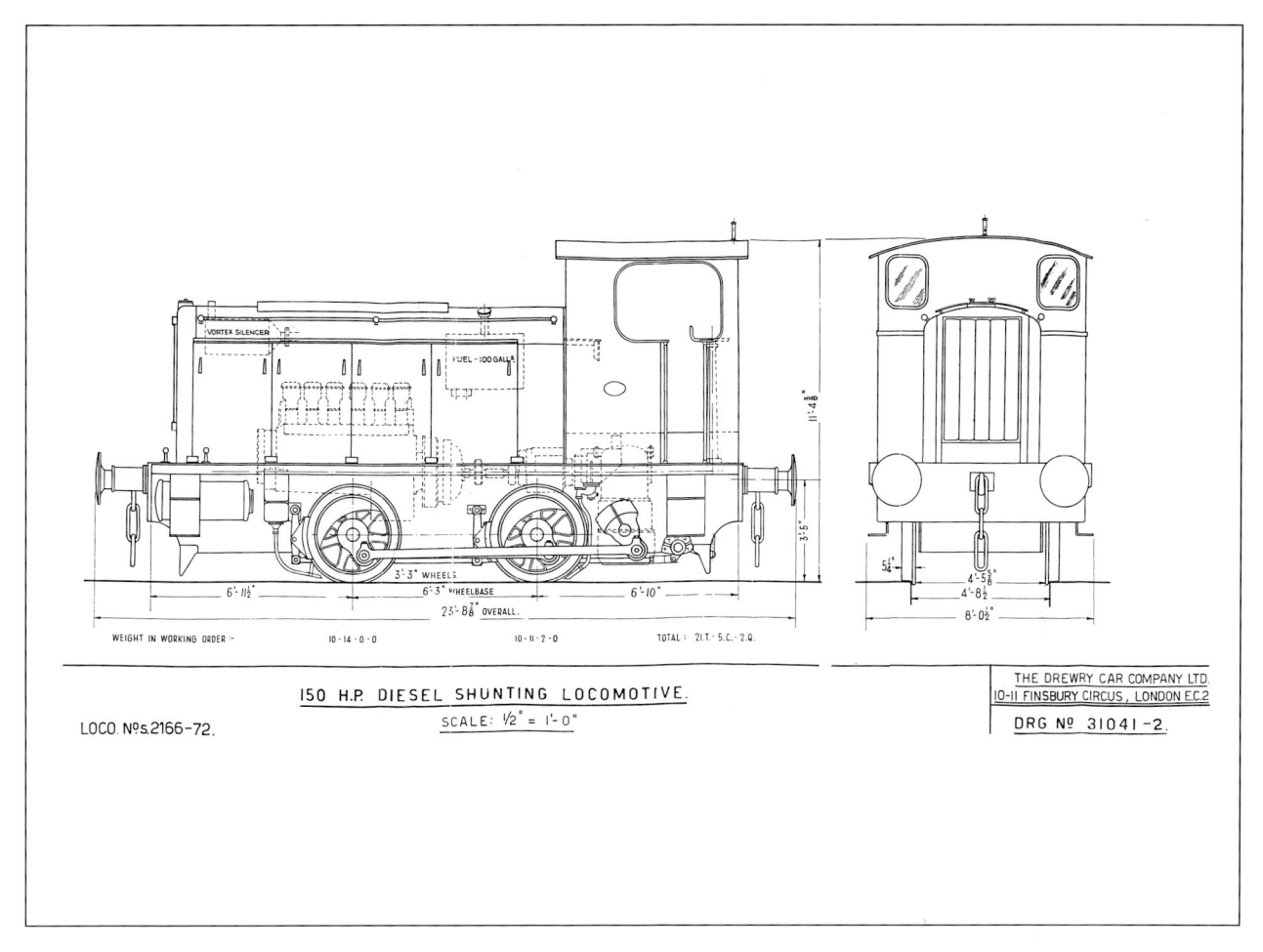

General arrangement of the Drewrys

The arrival of 'new' motive power to the Dockyard on 5 March 1993, with the transfer of MOD Army Drewry Nos 230 and 249, both of which had train air braking systems fitted by the Yorkshire Engine Co. Ltd. especially for use in Devonport Dockyard.
P. BURKHALTER

113

From left to right are 5199, 4858, 4860, 249 & 230 after the Drewry locos had been commissioned into service on 29 March 1993. P. BURKHALTER

Commissioning day for the Drewrys on 29 March 1993 comprised a run into North Yard to test clearances. P. BURKHALTER

Drewry 230 (DC2184/VF5265) seen shunting in the exchange sidings in June 1995. The unusual vehicle being propelled is a Scotrail engineer's inpection saloon on hire to MOD.
DEVONPORT MANAGEMENT LIMITED

original War Dept identity was 72222, then in a 1951 renumbering scheme it was given 831, but once again a new number was allocated in 1968 which was 249. Upon arrival in the Dockyard the Yard No was 10433. A plate is also carried indicating the work of fitting train air-braking in 1993: 'Yorkshire Engine Co. Ltd. Reworked 1993 L121'

It was supplied new on 26 July 1945 to the military depot at Steventon, Oxfordshire, and subsequently worked at a number of military sites, including Ludgershall, Tidworth, Bicester, Lockerley, Ashchurch, Ruddington, Eskmeals and Long Marston. In May 1968, whilst at Bicester, a new Gardiner engine of 195hp was fitted and it was at Long Marston that air braking was installed.

2184 (Vulcan works No 5265) has also carried a variety of numbers since new. Its original War Dept identity was 72229, then the 1951 renumbering scheme gave it 838, and in 1968 No 230 was allocated. Upon arrival in the Dockyard the Yard No was 10432. It also carries a plate indicating the air-brake fitting in 1993: 'Yorkshire Engine Co. Ltd. Reworked 1993 L120'

Supplied new on 26 September 1945 to the depot at Moreton on Lugg, 10432 moves paralleled 10433 being at, at various times, Bicester, Sterling, Ashford, Kent, Hereford and Long Marston. Like 10433 a new Gardiner engine was fitted at Bicester, in October 1964, whilst receiving a general overhaul.

10432 returned briefly to Long Marston between 2 and 22 March 1995, where Yorkshire Engine upgraded the train air-braking compressors. 10433 was similarly treated between 6 and 26 September 1995.

FALCON ENGINE & CAR WORKS LTD.

An engine was said to have been supplied to the Admiralty in 1884 (certainly they are listed as a customer in later catalogues) and could have been No 5. If it was, then it is likely to have been written off after the tunnel collision in July 1907, as contemporary reports say 'both ends of the locomotive were smashed. The chimney had been broken off in coming into contact with the roof [of the tunnel]. In fact No 5 was a total wreck'.

The mysterious John Fowler, works number 7710, delivered in December 1896 and of which nothing was subsequently heard!
RURAL HISTORY CENTRE, UNIVERSITY OF READING

JOHN FOWLER & CO.

7710: In January 1897 the Admiralty was supplied a new locomotive for Devonport, works number 7710. It was photographed in the works on 16 December 1896, but seems never to have carried a Dockyard number. Indeed it has vanished from sight as no later mention has ever been made of it.

F. C. HIBBERD & Co. Ltd.

In the 1950s the Admiralty purchased, for establishments all over Britain, thirty-three Hibberd type 'AD' standard gauge diesel locomotives, all of which had Foden engines and fluid drive couplings. This company used the trade name PLANET for its products, hence this title has been in common use in the Dockyard when referring to these locomotives. Drive to the wheels was by chains to internal shafts, so eliminating side coupling rods. Twenty-eight were delivered between 1955 and 1957, and of these ten went to Devonport. The Foden engines developed 105 hp and were all flameproofed for working in dangerous areas, though why this was applied to the Dockyard with all its hot metalwork equipment around is difficult to understand. The short wheelbase of 5 feet 6 inches enabled curves of 60 feet radius to be negotiated, and an overall length of 18 feet 2 inches kept the overhang to a minimum. These engines were the replacements for the steam fleet, although it can be seen that this was not implemented immediately.

3737: Delivered March 1957, and given Yard No 4856. Mainly saw service in North Yard apart from a reported brief loan to RNAD Ernesettle in July 1960. Sold to George Cohen on 3 December 1970, whence it went to Wagon Repairs at Gloucester. By 1990 this works had closed, and 3737 moved later that year to Marcroft Engineering (successors to Wagon Repairs), Port Tennant, Swansea. By April 1992 the loco was out of use and finally scrapped on site in November 1993.

3741: Arrived on site in May 1955 to receive Yard No 4857. In 1956 it collided with a car by St Levans Gate (the car coming off worse) but then had a uneventful career in North Yard until being scrapped on site in 1977.

3744: July 1955 saw the arrival of the third diesel, which was then numbered 4858. Chassis number was 2127. It was generally

A southbound passenger train at Central Offices stop in June 1965 with an unidentified Hibberd Planet in charge. To the left of the loco is the side of the North Yard loco shed. Here the driver will collect the single line staff to allow the train to enter the tunnel.
R HATELEY

one of the South Yard based locomotives, until the tunnel closed in 1982. At the grand old age of 37 years this, and 4860, were the last two operational Planets, finally being taken out of service on 29 March 1993, when the Drewrys (ten years older) became operational. The Defence Sales Organisation of the MoD offered them up for sale by tender in July 1993, and 4858 was purchased by J. Wells & Son of Portchester, Hants. It was removed on 3 December 1993, complete with Yard and Works plates. Its eventual fate remains a mystery.

3746: Delivered in August 1955 and allocated Yard No 4859. Sold, with 3737, in December 1970 to Cohens, then also going to Wagon Repairs.

3747 and **3774**: Total confusion with these two, as somewhere along the way the Yard numbers have been swapped around, or some records have not been as accurate as they should have been.

Delivered new in August 1955, the original records indicate that 3747 carried Yard No 4860, however at some stage it became Yard No 5198. On the other hand 3774 arrived in February 1956 to carry 5198, and then changed to 4860. The chassis number of 3774 is 2149. Fortunately both locomotives survived to come under the scrutiny of the author so their latter day identities are undisputed.

3747 was transferred in August 1984 to the NATO Mooring and Support Depot at Fairlie, Strathclyde, where it worked until being offered for disposal in January 1992. A group of enthusiasts based at the Caledonian Railway at Brechin purchased 3747, and it

Many mishaps occur, particularly due to road traffic occupying the same space as the railway. Here Planet Yard No 3741 has crashed into a car (or perhaps the other way round!) at St Levans in 1956. PLYMOUTH NAVAL BASE MUSEUM

117

Yard No 4858 in August 1972.
COLLECTION P. BURKHALTER

A memorable day for driver Dave Rogers on 17 February 1993, his last on the footplate of No 4858 before retirement.
P. BURKHALTER

moved again on 27 March 1992.

The highlight of 3774's career in the Dockyard, was to have the (dubious) honour of the last movement through the tunnel. On 10 November 1982, decorated with bunting and flags, and driven by Dave Rogers, it was met at the north end by the Port Admiral, who received the token staff from driver Rogers. As mentioned for 3744, the final date in operation for 3774 was 29 March 1993. Together with 3775, 3744 was sold to the Festiniog Railway to be used as a source of spares for their narrow gauge Hibberd. They left on two road trucks of P. H. Antell & Son on 7 October 1993 for breaking up at Farrington Gurney near Bristol.

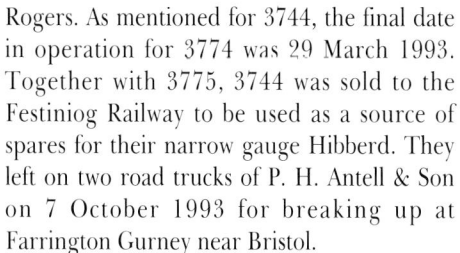

3773: New in February 1956, it was scrapped on site about 1980, and carried Yard No 5197.

3774: See 3747.

3775: Arrived on site March 1956, to be allocated Yard No 5199, it had been withdrawn from service by 1987 but was retained to provide a spares supply, although it is not believed to have been used as such. The chassis number is 2150. The Defence Sales Organisation of the MoD offered it up for sale by tender in July 1993, and the Festiniog Railway purchased it together with 3774 as a source of spares for their own narrow gauge Hibberd Planet. With 3774 it

THE LOCOMOTIVES

Photographed in 1956 when new, Yard No 4859 hauls a lengthy goods northbound outside the Central Offices, past No.2 on the extreme right.
P BRIDDON COLLECTION

F Hibberd & Co. 'Planet' diesel locomotives Yard Nos 4858 and 4860 photographed here in February 1992 in the Sidings. Both were still in use at that time. DEVONPORT MANAGEMENT LTD.

The 'Planets', as they were popularly known had oversize buffer plates to avoid buffer lock on the tight curves of the Dockyard. Here 5199 stands in the sidings in 1992, having been out of use for some years. DEVONPORT MANAGEMENT LTD.

The makers and Yard plates off FC Hibberd loco works number 3775. P. BURKHALTER

Double headed Planets haul a BR freight through the barracks grounds from Keyham Junction to the Exchange Sidings in June 1975. C HORSHAM

left on 7 October 1993 for breaking up at Farrington Gurney near Bristol.

3776: Delivered March 1956, with 5200 being allocated as the Yard number. On Friday 4 June 1982, at 8.30 a.m., a runaway wagon ran down the hill from Keyham Junction. Although a warning was telephoned through to the sidings, it was too late, and the wagon ran into 5200, pushing it 109 feet before stopping. Driver Cedric Whitrow had attempted to move to match the speed but had insufficient time before the impact. The regular driver was on holiday at the time and was most upset upon his return to find his loco written off. The locomotive was subsequently declared beyond repair, and sold to the Cornwall Railway Museum (Zelah) where it went on 6 April 1983. However in April 1987 it moved from there to be stood on a short length of track at the site of St Agnes Station (GWR) on the long closed Newquay to Chacewater line, outside the premises of Metal Protection Services Ltd. It has its engine started up now and again, although Dockyard sources recall that the crash rendered it unusable.

3816: The last of the line for Devonport, delivered May 1956. Given Yard No 5332, it usually operated in South Yard. It went off-site in the sale to G. Cohen in December 1970, and thence to Wagon Repairs.

So 1993 saw the end of this lengthy association with the Hibberd Planet diesels.

120

HAWTHORN LESLIE & CO.

2329: Supplied new to Sir John Jackson in February 1896, it can be surmised that it was obtained for the recently awarded Keyham contract, although no delivery location was shown in the manufacturer's books. The only subsequent mention is a report in 1899 that indicates a Hawthorn Leslie locomotive was on the site.

2399 and **2400**: Ordered by the Lords of the Admiralty for Devonport in June 1898 at a cost of £770 each, they were delivered in February 1899, and received Nos 1 and 2 respectively. Quite why they started this numbering scheme at this time is not known, as there were already the Fowler, possibly the Falcon, and maybe still the Aveling & Porter. They were put to use on the passenger service, and No 1 had the honour of hauling the Dockyard 'Royal Train' on 8 March 1902. At least No 1 had been reboilered by 1927 but in late 1948 it broke its rear axle, and both were taken out of service to be broken up on site. The commemorative plaque which recorded the Royal connection, plus the special royal coat-of-arms cast for the cab sides, were preserved and remain on display in the Dockyard Museum.

2599: One of the many crane tanks built by Hawthorn Leslie, it was sent off from the works on 29 December 1904. The single numeral 6 was carried on a circular plate on the cab sides. The crane capacity was 4 tons but the loco was converted to a conventional tank with a new boiler and side tanks in the Dockyard's own workshops sometime in the 1930s. It saw duty mainly in South Yard and

At its half century in 1948, Dockyard No 1 is polished up and bearing its Royal Crest outside the North Yard loco shed.
COLLECTION P. BURKHALTER

The Dockyard passenger train has conveyed Royalty once, on 8 March 1902. Here driver R R H Palk proudly poses with his engine outside Central Offices in North Yard. PLYMOUTH NAVAL BASE MUSEUM

Still on display in the Plymouth Naval Base Museum are both Royal Crests from loco No 1 P. BURKHALTER

This rare early view of No 2 and the passenger train in 1901. It would have just emerged from the tunnel into North Yard. FRANK JONES/ ARMY & NAVY ILLUSTRATED

was photographed there in 1951. It was finally scrapped in 1955.

2820 and **2821**: Both ordered on 15 January 1910, they were shipped together on 16 June the same year. Allocated 7 and 8 in the engine number series, they were seen operating the passenger service in 1951. Both were withdrawn from railway service in 1955, but were then put to use as stationary steam boilers; No 8 being located outside No 2 shop.

3200 and **3201**: Again a double order by the Admiralty, this time in 1916. These two were given numbers 14 and 15 and saw service on all the Dockyard duties, until withdrawal in 1955 and 1956. 14 later was put to good use as a portable boiler. No 15 was scrapped in the Yard in 1956

HUGHES LOCOMOTIVE & TRAMWAY ENGINE WORKS LTD.

340: Built in 1880 this could have been No 4 in the Admiralty fleet, and there is the surmise that it was acquired with Barclays 296 from Sir John Jackson at the end of the Contract. The newspaper reports of these sales are however silent on this item.

THE LOCOMOTIVES

No 6 started off as a crane locomotive, but was converted in the 1930s in the Dockyard workshops. Here seen on 25 May 1951 with a full crew compliment. PLYMOUTH NAVAL BASE MUSEUM

The southbound passenger at St Levans about to enter the 'Narrows' on 28 September 1951, behind Hawthorn Leslie 2820, No 7.
HAROLD D BOWTELL

Many of the steam locomotives found use as stationary steam raising plants after their haulage days had passed. Here No 14 stands off the rails in the 1950s. B MENNIE

Hudswell Clarke & Co. works number 287, built in 1887, came to Jackson's Keyham contract in January 1900 before travelling with him to a job in Spain after Keyham had finished. F JONES

HUDSWELL CLARKE & CO. LTD.

287: Popularly known as *Maggie* for all its life, it was delivered on 12 November 1887 to William P. Hartley (the jam manufacturer) at Aintree Liverpool. It did not last long here for in March 1895 they sold it onto the Electo-Chemical Co. Ltd. of St Helens. Once again the ownership was short-lived as it seems that they traded *Maggie* in with Pecketts of Bristol for a new locomotive in September 1898. It remained with Pecketts until 27 January 1900, when they sold it to Jackson for £600. This sale has been recorded for posterity in

124

the correspondence files and forms a delightful exchange. I am grateful particularly to K. P. Plant for documenting this in the *Industrial Railway Record*, and I quote from his article:

> We note in the Contract Journal that you have a tank locomotive 10in cylinder four wheel coupled for sale and we should be obliged to receive from you full particulars and photograph at your convenience.

So wrote John J. Warbrick, Secretary of Sir John Jackson Ltd. of 3 Victoria Street, Westminster, London, to Peckett & Sons on 9 November 1899. They replied by return and were advised that 'Sir John Jackson is away in the North at present but we expect him back in Town about the middle or end of next week when your letter shall be placed before him'. However, on the 15th Jackson's indicated that their 'Mechanical Engineer (Mr Prechous) from Keyham will no doubt call upon you to inspect the loco *Maggie* at an early date'. It was from Keyham that Geo. H. Scott wrote the following day to say that their 'Mr. Prechous will be in Bristol on Monday morning next to inspect this engine. Kindly arrange to have cylinder and slide valve covers off and ash pan and fire bars removed ready for his inspection.' Prechous was obviously impressed with 'the 10in loco *Maggie* by Hudswell Clarke' and when Scott wrote to Pecketts on 8th January he indicated that she was 'an engine that would suit us at a moderate price. Mr. Prechous tells me you ask as much as £625, delivered to London or equal thereto, which is as much as we paid for 10in cylinders new not so very long ago. We do not see our way to go quite to this figure but we do make you a firm offer of £550 nett cash during month following delivery at these works. You of course to find lamps as promised.' Peckett's were not prepared to drop as low as £550 and suggested £600. Agreement was evidently reached as Maggie left for Keyham on 27 January 1900.

Hudswell Clarke's records have annotated that in 1910 it was with Sir John Jackson in Ferrol (Spain), then S. Pearson & Son (contractors) at the Gretna (Munitions Factory) in 1916. Again a short-lived home as by 1919 it was at the Gas Light & Coke Co. in Becton, east London, as their No 37.

293: Purchased by T. A. Walker, the contractor for the massive Manchester Ship Canal works, and left Hudswell Clarke's works on 30 December 1887 for Irlam, carrying the name *Flixton*. Jackson's no doubt picked her up after taking on some of this job after Walker's crashed, although it is believed that she was not actually owned by Jackson at the canal.

318: Also bought by Walker, this one left Leeds named *Heaton* on 21 February 1889 for the No 1 section of the canal works. It presumably arrived at Devonport in the same manner as 293, and was renamed (un-originally) *Keyham*. Later John Griffiths & Son Ltd. of Liverpool owned her, and by 1921 she was in the hands of Firth Blakeley Son & Co. at Church Fenton.

HUNSLET ENGINE WORKS

1: Those in the know, in industrial locomotive history circles, will well appreciate the shaky ground that the author is about to enter. The history of this particular engine, and that of Hunslet works number 401, has been the subject of endless debate for years. What is about to follow is a distillation of various sources into a 'best guess' scenario.

As can be readily surmised, this was Hunslet's first venture. Construction commenced in about the summer of 1864 and it left the works on 18 July 1865 bound for the railway contractors Brassey & Ballard on their contract for the Midland Railway south of Bedford. At this time it bore the name *Linden*. By 1878 she was owned by J. P. Edwards, another contractor with work in the Nottingham area and the same name was given the locomotive. However in 1888 T. A. Walker had her, by now carrying the title *Patricroft*, and as he already had another engine of the same name, bestowed her with *Swansea*. Like many others at the Manchester Canal she passed into the hands of John Jackson. Certainly in May 1902 Hunslet supplied Jackson with spares, probably to Devonport. At the auction the bidding went to

Hunslet Engine Co. No 1, almost one hundred years old in 1961 at Sharlston Colliery.
R Hateley

£240 but Jackson still had her in 1909. Indeed the next years are clouded in mystery until she turned up at the Dagenham Docks site of Samuel Williams, as their No 6. She ended her days at Sharlston Colliery where her significance had not been realised before being cut up at the end of 1965, a full one hundred years old.

360: 'Sent away' from Leeds on the last day of 1884 carrying the name *Lytham* to T. A. Walker at Manchester, and again ended up with Jackson at Devonport, with the very original name of *Tamar*. As spares were supplied to Keyham as late as January 1906 she seems to have seen the job almost all the way through. Later in life, in about 1923, her owner was H. Covington & Sons at Battersea.

401: Another F. A. Walker purchase, this one delivered on 8 July 1886 with the name *Gloucester*. Hunslet records indicate that this engine was in Jackson's hands by September 1898, but confusingly also records that spares were delivered to Dover in 1904, which contract Jackson had finished in 1902. This could be a northerner's confusion; Dover instead of Devonport, in the same way as Portsmouth gets mixed up with Plymouth. Certainly the loco was in the end of contract sale at Keyham on 31 January 1907, when the auctioneer started the bidding for the 'recently re-tubed' *Devonport* at £100 but only reaching £170 before being withdrawn. Jackson then used her at Amesbury after a sojourn at his plant depot at Grays in Essex. By 1917 she was in the hands of Samuel Williams & Co., the operators of Dagenham Docks, becoming their No 6. (but see HE 1 above.) It was sold on in October 1949 to the National Coal Board in Barnsley. There has been confusion between this engine and Hunslet's No 1, and there could have been a boiler switch between the two, maybe in the workshops at Devonport.

437: Also Walker's in 1887, named *Manchester*, but Hunslet supplied spares to Keyham in September 1900 and August 1905. The sale reports have it that she was sold for £375 on 30 January 1907, but she re-appears in the books at Jackson's Grays Depot in 1921. Perhaps the purchaser failed to come up with the cash.

THE LOCOMOTIVES

MANNING WARDLE

714: Of Manning Wardle's class E and ex-works on 24 January 1879, it was bought by T. A. Walker for his contract at Deal in Kent and named *Martin*. It moved on with Walker to the Manchester Ship Canal, then passed into Jackson's hands. Somewhere along the line the name *Clyde* became used. The auctioneer knocked it down for £91 on 30 January 1907, the price indicating perhaps scrap value only.

951: Purchased by Logan & Hemmingway (a railway contractor), this class Q left Leeds on 7 January 1885 for the canal works at Openshaw. Later sold onto T. A. Walker when it carried Accrington on a brass plate in 3¾ inch letters. It came into Manning Wardle's works for repairs in October 1888, when a cab canopy was fitted. It arrived at Keyham with other ex-Ship Canal engines in May 1898 and in October 1900, at the extensive site workshops that Jackson had installed, the boiler was extensively rebuilt. In the months that followed various minor repairs were made but, catastrophically, the maintenance was not as it should have been, and a tube burst on the morning of 3 November 1902. The fireman jumped off the footplate but became entangled in the truck wheels and was instantly killed. Full details of this incident appears on page 51. The Board of Trade Surveyor found that an inspection of the tubes on the fifteenth of the previous month resulted in a new set being ordered, as they were deemed suspect. The locomotive had been scheduled to go into the workshops on 8 November for re-tubing, but events overtook this decision. It is obvious that the ordered replacement tubes were eventually used, as in the end of contract sale the good price of £475 was reached, but a sale was not proceeded with as it was still in Jackson's

The only known photograph of this locomotive, Manning Wardle works number 714, which on Jackson's site carried the nameplate CLYDE. Here seen on the floor of the Entrance Lock to the closed basin on 18 July 1903. PUBLIC RECORD OFFICE ADM195/61

Here photographed at Dagenham Docks by Ivo Peters in the 1950s, Manning Wardle works number 951 left the manufacturer in 1885. In Jackson's hands at Devonport it blew a tube, and as a result the fireman was killed. PHOTOGRAPH BY IVO PETERS, COURTESY JULIAN PETERS

hands at his Grays Depot until being offered for sale in August 1921. Sometime after leaving Keyham it gained the name Devonport. It then went to Samuel Williams at Dagenham Docks, and was still in use there in 1950.

1018: One of the wider travelled locomotives to have been associated with Devonport, this class F was delivered to Liverpool Docks on 9 May 1887 for T. A. Walker's Buenos Aires contract in Argentina, being suitably named *Ocantes*. By 1897 it was back in England and working for the contractor Pauling's & Co. on their job building the line from Stert Junction to Westbury for the Great Western Railway. It is probable that Pauling's sold her to Jackson in April 1900, by which time the very English name of *Lord Roberts* was in place. Manning Wardle supplied a new copper firebox from stock on 6 July 1904, but no further mention appears, except that the sale report has an engine *Lord Kitchener* sold for £210, could this be a reporter's mishearing of the name?

1036: Another class F for Walker's but this one went no further than the Ship Canal on 3 November 1887, carrying *Barham* on the regulation brass plate. On arrival at Devonport *Torcross* was the given name to reflect the village in South Devon off which the stone for the concrete was dredged. It fetched £130 at the end of the works, and moved onto Cochrane & Co. (Annan), until about 1918 when the Air Ministry had her at their Kidbrooke site. After 1937 she moved to Sealand, Flint, finally disappearing (probably scrapped) by 1952, at the grand old age of 65.

1051: Class F in Manning Wardle's classification, first put into steam in the workshops in Leeds on 27 January 1888 and then dispatched the following day. Named *Canterbury* for T. A. Walker's Manchester Ship Canal job, she ended up in John Jackson's hands with the name *Tyne*. This indicates that she may have put in service on Jackson's Tynemouth pier contract before coming to Devonport. Certainly she came up for sale at the Keyham auction on 31 January 1907, when the bidding went up to £215 after starting at £100. No later history has yet come to light.

1090: A class H 'sent away' from Leeds on 19 December 1888 to T. A. Walker at Manchester and called *Cadishead*. In Jackson's hands she was named *Lord Nelson*, and was sold for £310 in January 1907.

1342: The contractor Pauling & Co. took delivery of this class F on 4 June 1897 for their Westbury contract as *Westminster No 10*. Possibly at the same time as No 1018 she came to John Jackson, and was given the very parochial name *Mount Edgcumbe*. Somewhat surprisingly no later information appears to have survived for this very new engine.

RANSOMES & RAPIER

On 17 January 1939 they shipped three small 2 feet gauge 20hp locomotives of $3\frac{1}{4}$ tons each (works Nos 85, 89 and 90), to Bernard Sunley & Co. at Plymouth. This was possibly for the same contract as the Wingrove & Rogers loco's mentioned later.

RUSTON & HORNSBY

For the No 10 Dock widening contract by Edmund Nuttall, Sons & Co. (London) Ltd., works numbers 186314 and 186316 were delivered on 14 and 21 August 1937. These were of the 44/48 BHP class of shunting locomotives weighing $7\frac{1}{2}$ tons. By September 1939 RH186316 had moved to a contract at the Royal Ordnance Factory, Glascoed, and in May 1940 186314 had been returned to Nuttall's plant depot at Colnbrook, Slough.

SHARP STEWART & CO.

3474: T. A. Walker placed an order in February 1888 for five large six-wheel engines which were to be delivered in four and a half months. In this batch was *Openshaw*, works No 3474 and the works record for 2 August 1888 lists this and the other four (*Knutsford, Tatton, Northwich* and *Stalybridge*). If this locomotive was at Keyham, it would have been somewhat larger than all the other here. Subsequently it was in store at the Grays Yard, and when Thomas W. Ward Ltd. purchased this site in

Another presumed locomotive with Jackson was Sharp Stewart No 3474 OPENSHAW, though this fine works photograph may have been of a similar engine, with a different name painted on the negative plate. GLASGOW LIBRARY SERVICES

1924, they picked up some of the equipment there as well, including this engine. Ward's advertised it for sale in December 1926 at £450, but still had it in lists in later years. It disappeared after August 1935, presumably cut up.

STRACHAN & HENSHAW LTD.

This Bristol based mechanical engineering company has ventured into the railway world from time to time, and in 1967 produced a line of twelve Trackmobile's under licence from the Whiting Corporation, Illinois, USA. The 'right-angled' road/rail system is somewhat novel, but is still being offered by Trackmobile in the 1990s. The traction on the rails is provided by a weight transfer system from the rail vehicle being hauled.

7503: Supplied to the Navy at Devonport in 1967 painted yellow. Due to the gradient at the sidings its haulage power was severely limited and it became a bit of a joke. Before too long, 3 March 1969 to be precise, it was transferred to Portsmouth Dockyard. After the rail system in that dockyard closed in December 1977 it languished off the rails, the last documented enthusiast sighting being on 29 August 1978.

7510: Somewhat ironically another of these machines turned up at Devonport, but much later. As has been mentioned elsewhere, Grant Lyon Eagre Ltd, the railway contractors of Scunthorpe, carried out a refurbishment contract in 1992, and in March brought to the site this unit in almost original condition. It distinguished itself by becoming detached from the ballast wagon it was hauling, which ran down the hill and into a parked van. This latter vehicle was owned by a demolition contractor and it was difficult to identify the exact damage caused, from all the other bodywork defects.

Pictured on Navy Days August 1978 at Portsmouth, the Strachan & Henshaw works number 7503 Trackmobile type road/rail unit which saw little use in Devonport before being transferred. I BENDALL

RNAD Ernesettle loaned the Dockyard one of their Unimog road/rail tractors in June 1992 for trials. Here 52 RN 33 is seen attached to five VGA vans and the scrap class 47 (47538), just to make it really difficult!
DEVONPORT MANAGEMENT LTD.

UNIMOG

A Mercedes adaptation of a road truck which has small rail wheels but which are only for guidance, the traction being provided by the rubber road tyres on the track. The Ministry of Defence purchased this unit (Registration No 52-RN-33) for RNAD Ernesettle, just up the River Tamar above the Tamar Road Bridge. It has made rare appearances at Devonport for specific needs, mainly in connection with its train air braking capability. Confirmed visits were 23 June and 3 July 1992

WINGROVE & ROGERS

Just before the war the contractors Bernard Sunley & Co. Ltd. carried out a reservoir construction contract for the Admiralty at Devonport where three small battery electric locomotives of 2 feet gauge were employed (works Nos 1395 to 1397).

CHAPTER FOURTEEN
ROLLING STOCK

The original reason for the existence of a railway in the Yards of Devonport and Keyham was to facilitate the movement of goods to and around the various workshops, stores, wharves and docks. Later came the additional service of a passenger train, like the freight, solely devoted to internal movements.

For both these purposes, the railway had its own fleet of vehicles and, due to the customary approach of self-sufficiency, they were rebuilt in the Yard's own workshops from secondhand wagons. At regular intervals the Dockyard would buy up redundant main line wagons and use the frames to construct their own vehicles, this work being done at the Joiners' Shop in North Yard. On the railway siding to the west of the Shop they were stripped of the redundant original body and mechanical parts were removed for refurbishment. As a consequence the whole area was littered with wheelsets and springs.

Springs would be sent to the smiths for repair and the axleboxes to the fitters' shop, before all being put back together. The chassis would be run into a bay siding leading into the building, via a turntable. Here a main frame of oak and elm would be made and fitted, elm being used for the curved members, and the sides and roof made of tongued and grooved boarding, the roof being covered in felt. The livery carried was a light (or battleship) grey, although there is some indication of the usage of service green and blue as well. Each vehicle took about six weeks to complete, coaches longer due to the extra work. As there were often a large number of wagons awaiting attention in a long line it was no wonder the wheelwrights' saying was 'job for life'. Some wagons had been there so long grass was growing around the wheels. With the gradual decline of rail traffic this wagon building ceased about 1966.

The origins of the wagons are obscure

Workmen's coach No 1 in a train at Central Offices c1956.
HUGH DAVIES

Snow lies on the ground as the passenger train heads north on the line adjacent to the Exchange Sidings in January 1963.
P. GRAY

and no fleet records have survived. Sporadic reports state that just after the Second World War wagons with GER on the axleboxes were recorded and two noted in 1961 were Cravens (1916) and Ashbury.

PASSENGER CARRIAGES

Two rakes of coaches were provided, each rake comprising six carriages; four for the workmen and two differing types for the officers. On occasions trains were run with one fewer coach, presumably when they were withdrawn for maintenance. A flat bed four-wheel freight wagon was attached to each rake to provide space for tool boxes, light goods and materials, even bicycles, being conveyed by passengers. Generally coaches were 19 feet long and 7 feet 8 inches wide, with the roof height of about 9 feet to clear the tunnel. Each train, including locomotive, was 157 feet in length. The coaches were fitted with permanent wooden steps for entry and dismounting. As described earlier there were six classes of accommodation for passengers, as follows:

	Capacity		
	Sitting	Standing	
Admiral Superintendent & Principal Officers	8	-	
Superior & Commissioned Officers	10	-	} one coach per train
Subordinate Officers	10	-	
Recorders	11	-	
Chargemen (i.e. Foremen)	11	-	} one coach per train
CPOs & POs	10	-	
Workmen	24	10	four coaches per train

Compartment coach No 16, which contained upholstered seats, overhead luggage racks, and was decorated with appropriate framed pictures c. 1956.
HUGH DAVIES

Workmen's coach No 344 had no glazing, no lighting, and a wooden bench seat around the perimeter. PLYMOUTH NAVAL BASE MUSEUM.

The total carrying capacity of the train was 196, 156 sitting and 40 standing, although the latter was an estimate only as there were no laid down rules in this respect.

The workmen's coach resembled a goods closed van with unglazed openings, which meant that the rain came in, except when in the tunnel in which case it was the smoke from the locomotive exhaust. For seating there were wooden benches around the interior of the body, and a half stable type door.

By contrast the officer classes' compartments were upholstered, with the only lighting provided in any coach in the Admiral Superintendent's section, supplied from a battery under the seat. Also in this compartment were two framed photographs

Coach No.342 contained the Admiral Superintendent's compartment (here on the right). This contained the only lighting on the train, and was normally locked, to prevent unauthorised use. PLYMOUTH NAVAL BASE MUSEUM

of the Terrace in South Yard before and after the Second World War blitz damage. Other decoration was provided by pictures of ships and mirrors. A net luggage rack over the seats in the upholstered classes completed the standard layout.

Whilst the coach frames were fitted with sprung buffers the coupling was a loose three link chain. This resulted in a very rough passage on setting off as the drivers were known just to fully open the throttle wide without taking up any slack showing little regard for the comfort of the passengers.

The passenger coaches were examined every Friday by a wheelwright and a joiner, and greased and cleaned at the same time. Defects were either remedied at the same time, if small, or the Constructive Department were asked to undertake work that was too large for a running repair. For both freight and passenger stock an annual inspection and a biennial test of couplings were obligatory.

Photographic evidence over the life of the passenger service reveals a variety of designs for the passenger coaches. The first compartment carriages in 1902 had single sided seating in each compartment whereas after the Second World War more conventional double seating is apparent. In addition, rebuilding was undertaken, for example photographs of coach number 16 taken in 1956 and 1965 show quite differing construction.

At the end of the passenger service the stoutly constructed carriages seemed to be in demand as an un-named transport museum offered to purchase some of them. However it is not believed that this came about. It was also said that a road contractor bought some for use as site cabins. At the time of writing a plan exists to re-create one for the Historic Dockyard at Chatham in Kent to convey visitors around the site, but it has not yet reached fruition.

Closed wagon No. 58 with panel sides. Note the low profile roof to allow use through the tunnel. PLYMOUTH NAVAL BASE MUSEUM

FREIGHT WAGONS

The freight rolling stock comprised a remarkable collection of vehicles for a wide range of purposes. Goods carried were as varied as one could imagine; timber baulks in long lengths on bogie bolsters, perishable stores in closed vans, heavy test weights on multi-wheel flat wagons, the list is endless. No full stock list has been found, hence any listing is therefore incomplete, and nothing is known of the very early rolling stock.

One use of closed vans, which from time to time received official disapproval, was as a tradesmen's store-van and 'bunk'. This would be moved with the gang to beside whichever ship they were working on and would contain tools, plus be a 'resting place'. Every so often the numbers of such vans grew to such a proportion that shortages of van availability occurred and facilities were withdrawn.

Some high vans were marked clearly 'For North Yard Use Only'. An anecdote is related that prior to being so marked, some were sent into the tunnel with destructive results, hence the restriction on usage.

Even with the gradual run-down of freight service a report in 1976 stated that sixty-nine Dockyard wagons were in use.

After the tank wagon run-away incident described in on page 77 the Army Rail Organisation were requested to transfer brake van number 49004 to Devonport for use on goods trains. This van was built by the Southern Railway at its Ashford Works in 1942 as part of a War Office order. The vans were 25 ton vehicles to a basic SR design but with the addition of vacuum brakes with the cylinders unusually positioned above the frames. The van was specially adapted in the

Closed 10 ton van No 178, of plank construction PLYMOUTH NAVAL BASE MUSEUM

Closed 5 ton van No 419. Note the directive 'Not for tunnel working'. PLYMOUTH NAVAL BASE MUSEUM

7 plank open wagon No 451. PLYMOUTH NAVAL BASE MUSEUM

Yard's workshops to allow it to pass through the tunnel and at the same time the end vestibules were removed. A small metal plate records this work: 'This van was rebuilt by Ken Norwood and Neal Kingdom. Wheelwrights Shop Devonport Dockyard 1976'.

Most of the wagons disposed of at the end of service in the 1980s were acquired by the Plym Valley Railway, who are relaying rails for a distance of 1½ miles along the old GWR Tavistock and Launceston branch from Marsh Mills on the eastern outskirts of Plymouth. Almost 30 wagons of various types were acquired, although some have been scrapped since. However a selection have survived and are in use on the line. This includes the ex-SR brake van and one of the diesel rail cranes. See Appendix 6 for details.

40 ton flatbed, used for moving test weights around the Yard, here seen in South Yard with the ropery in the background. PLYMOUTH NAVAL BASE MUSEUM.

Double unit No 393 for conveying gun barrels. PLYMOUTH NAVAL BASE MUSEUM.

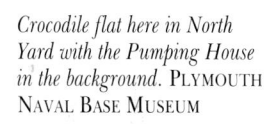

Crocodile flat here in North Yard with the Pumping House in the background. PLYMOUTH NAVAL BASE MUSEUM

Well wagon No 334, rated to carry 25 tons in the well area. Now preserved on the Plym Valley Railway. PLYMOUTH NAVAL BASE MUSEUM

Bogie tube wagon No 336 in South Yard, loaded with dock blocks. This vehicle stars in the film 'Force 10 from Navarone', but some actors unfortunately get in the way. PLYMOUTH NAVAL BASE MUSEUM.

SR built guard's van, altered in the Dockyard Joiners' Shop to allow use through the tunnel, when the end vestibules were also removed. Now preserved at the Plym Valley Railway.
P. BURKHALTER

CHAPTER FIFTEEN
RAILGAUGE SHUNTING CRANES

The rails of the Dockyard system were also used by self-propelled shunting cranes. These cranes carried very large timber buffers, which reached down to nearly track level, together with conventional 3-link drawgear. They were employed to carry out sundry lifts of equipment and for unloading trucks, which they could also shunt to the necessary location. Those in South Yard were for use in the timber yards, loading the logs onto bogie trucks for transportation to the Joiners' Shop in North Yard. They also lifted the trunks out of the timber ponds, and from the Camber, onto the low loader wagons, which they then hauled, or pushed, to the timber stacks.

The earliest recorded, in 1890, supplied by Grafton's of Vulcan Works, Bedford, was steam propelled from a vertical boiler on a four wheel chassis. Indeed steam was the motive power for all these cranes up to 1952, when the last of these was supplied by Grafton's also. Records are sketchy but there could have been nearly 80 steam lattice jib

Grafton Steam crane, works number 2597 of 1942, photographed in August 1972 to the south of 81 Shop in North Yard.
COLLECTION P. BURKHALTER

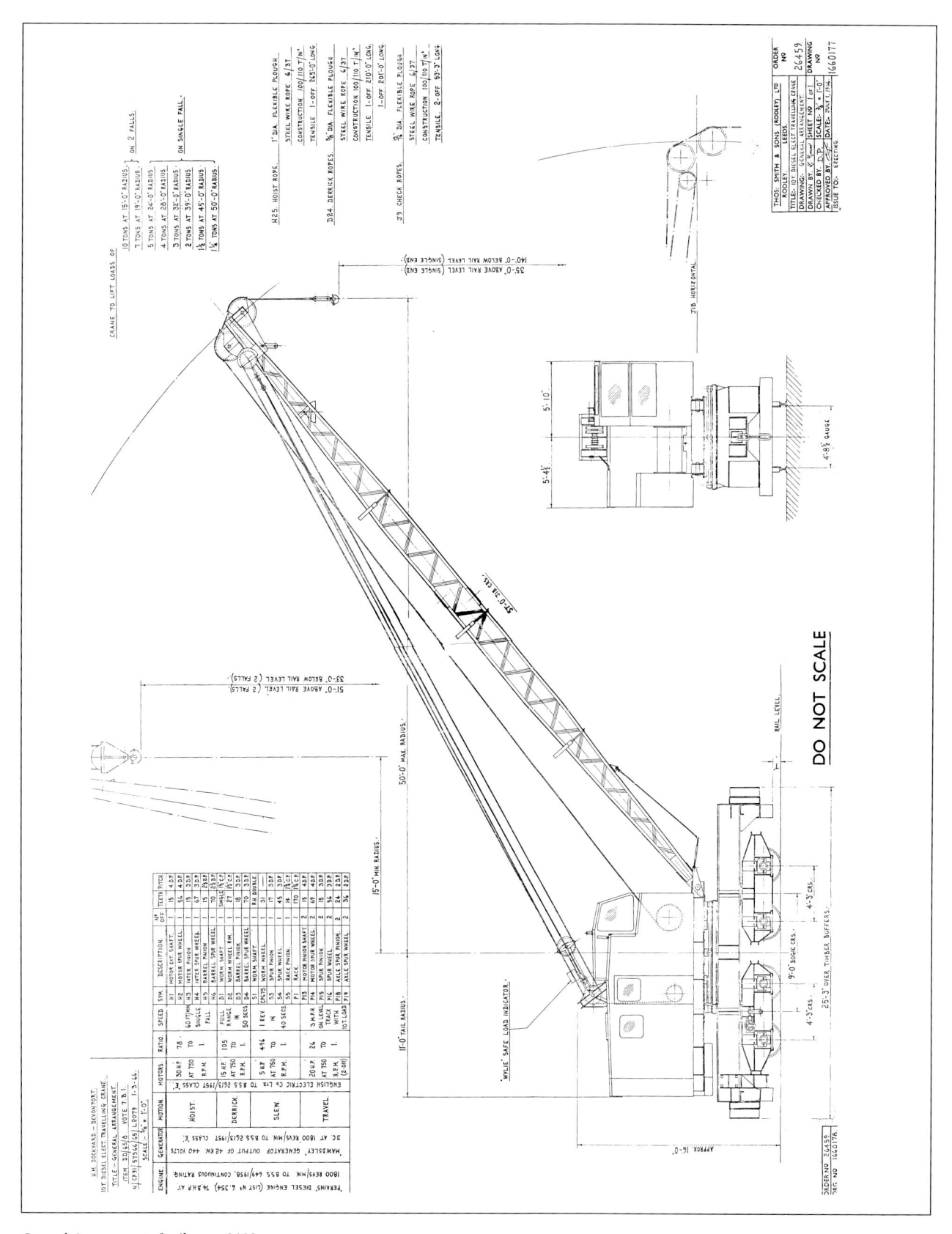

General Arrangement of rail crane 9103

cranes of up to 10 ton capacity. The steam cranes had a remarkable life span as the last one, Yard No 176 of 1940, also by Grafton's, survived until 1976 in South Yard, being taken out of service on 28 February of that year and scrapped.

One of the Dockyard steam cranes (identity unknown) ended up at the Royal Naval Air Station at Mount Batten, to the east of Plymouth Sound, where it was photographed c1917 lifting seaplanes into and out of the water.

Grafton's, which had the bulk of the Admiralty market, was formed in London in 1883, but soon moved to Bedford in 1886. It can be seen that the Admiralty Yards were early customers, but other manufacturers also had a share. Joseph Booth & Bros. Ltd. and T. Smith & Sons (Rodley) Ltd. both obtained orders whilst Coles, Taylor & Hubbard and Stothert & Pitt all delivered a few units each.

From 1952 onwards, however, diesel took over the motive power, although the basic design remained the same. This latter point was partly due to T. Smith & Sons (Rodley) Ltd. being the apparent sole supplier of twenty-nine up until 1968. Appendix Seven documents the known list of these units and their locations, as obviously they could not pass through the tunnel. Two transfers were known between North and South Yards but, as dismantling and haulage round through the adjacent streets would have been involved, it was a rare occurrence. The sizes were evenly split between three and six tons, with the very last two being of 10 tons capacity. In one instance, at least, a conversion from three to six tons was carried out on site, this being to Yard No 5188 in 1967. The last diesel rail crane lasted until 1990 in North Yard, although it had not been in use for some time.

The enormous batch of twenty-two cranes delivered between April and October 1956 cost the staggering sum of £192,589. Bear in mind that ten new Planet diesel locomotives were also delivered at this time and there must have been great pressure on the Yard fitters. The order was part of a very large consolidated one for a total of 32 cranes for all the Home Yards, plus one for Malta. This must have been good business for Smiths at their Leeds factory.

On 10 August 1966 *HMS Tiger* (of Wilson/Smith Rhodesia talks fame) was moored on No 10/11 wharf and during a gun test accidentally fired a six-inch dummy shell which bounced off the wharf edge into the underside of a steam crane, resulting in the crane being scrapped.

By 1977 the cranes were to be seen in use throughout South Yard and on the dock and basin side tracks in North Yard. Even as late as 1981 use was still being made of these units at various locations. Diesel crane 5193 was acquired by the Plym Valley Railway, and is in use on their line in the reconstruction of the railway at Marsh Mills, Plymouth.

The Contractor, Sir John Jackson, made use of steam cranes and navvys in his works, although they were primarily only used for lifting and not shunting. Between 1895 and 1898, T. Smith and J. Booth supplied twenty ordinary standard gauge cranes, with Booths delivering eight dual gauge (standard and broad) for use as navvys.

T. Smith & Sons (Rodley) Ltd. supplied a large number of diesel rail shunting cranes, and one has survived in the hands of the Plym Valley Railway, seen here in 1994 actively assisting in the rebuilding of part of the GWR Tavistock branch at Marsh Mills. P. BURKHALTER

APPENDIX ONE

TUNNEL BELL SIGNALS

COPY TO BE POSTED IN EACH SIGNAL BOX
INSTRUCTIONS IN USE OF PATENT COMBINED TRAIN STAFF AND BLOCK INSTRUMENTS
FOR
WORKING SINGLE LINES AS FITTED IN DOCKYARD SIGNAL BOXES
STATION A   ASSUMING A TRAIN IS GOING FROM A TO B   STATION B

The train staffs are locked up at A, and the key (so to speak) is in the hands of the signalman at B, who by means of an electric current, unlocks of the magazine at A, in which the train staffs are kept.

	Starting Train	Mode of working		Receiving Train	
1	Call attention	*	2.	Acknowledge	*
3	Send 'Warning' Signal	***	4.	If line is clear accept the train	****
5	Ask for Train Staff	******	6.	Acknowledge and	*
7	On receiving acknowledgement, immediately lift Staff into head of instrument and withdraw.		6a.	Hold down the ringing key thereby deflecting the galvanometer needle on both instrument.	
8	Turn left-hand indicator to 'Staff Out' pressing the indicator hard down until galvanometer needle returns to zero.		8a.	On seeing the galvanometer needle return to zero, release the key and turn left-hand indicator 'Staff Out'.	
9	Send 'Train on' Signal.	**	10.	Acknowledge	*
				On arrival of train	
			1.	Place Train Staff in magazine and turn left-hand indicator to 'Staff In'.	
3.	Acknowledge and turn left-hand indicator to 'Staff In'.	*	2.	Send 'Train Off' Signal	*

APPENDIX TWO

NAVY ESTIMATES 1854 to 1935

Year	£ in year	£ total est.	
1854/55	35,000		Estimate for tunnel
1855/56	10,000		Expenditure on tunnel
1856/57	25,000		Expenditure on tunnel
1857/58	2,911		Excess expenditure on tunnel
1867/68	520		Turntable, east wall of North Basin
1869/70	1,030		Extension of railway
1870/71	1,030		Extension of railway
1872/73	580		Interest on outlay for branch railway into Yard including (later) line through tunnel (this item appears each year until 1888)
1877	600		Forming narrow gauge in Yard
1878/79	6,000		Railways in Yard
1879/80	3,000		Railways in Yard
1880/81	3,000		Railways in Yard
1881/82	3,000		Railways in Yard

APPENDIX TWO
continued

Year	£ in year	£ total est.	
1882/83	4,000		Railways in Yard
1884/85	275		Railway from boiler shears into erecting shop
	275		Extension of railway into Boiler Shop
1885/86	215		Housing for locomotive (Keyham Yard)
1887/88	1,800		Railway round stores (Devonport), to facilitate transport
		400	Extension of railway north of Camber to bring wagons under the cranes.
		190	Lines of rails in Mast House (Keyham)
		220	Paving between railways (Keyham) to allow anchor trucks to cross.
1890/91	2,000	3,695	Pier with tramway at Barracks for landing and embarking purposes in connection with new barracks.
1892/93	1,000	2,800	Relaying main line of railway (Devonport)
1895/96	600	1,100	Machine Shop paving and railway (Devonport)
1898/99	1,000		Extension of railways to connect main line with various shops. (Keyham)
1899/00	2,000		Extension of railways
1900/01	1,000		Railway improvements in Devonport Yard.
1901/02	1,000	4,000	Railways in Devonport Yard
	1,000	1,700	Railways in Keyham Yard
1902/03	1,600	4,600	Railways in Devonport Yard
1903/04	1,300	4,100	Railways in Devonport Yard
	2,000	5,000	Railway lines round storehouses (Devonport)
1904/05	1,000	5,000	Railway lines round storehouses (Devonport)
	5,000	19,450	Railways in North & South Yards
	5,000	40,000	New jetty and railways at 2 & 3 slip in South Yard
1905/06	4,000	19,450	Railways in North & South Yards
1906/07	11,000	31,000	New jetty and railways at 2 & 3 slip in South Yard
	6,400	19,450	Railways in North & South Yards
1907/08	3,800	28,000	New jetty and railways at 2 & 3 slip in South Yard
1908/09	1,000	28,000	New jetty and railways at 2 & 3 slip in South Yard (completed in 1909)
1922/23	7,000	10,000	Renewal of railways
1924/25	1,000	15,000	Improving railways
1925/26	4,000	15,600	Ditto
1928	1,600	15,600	Ditto
1930	1,500	5,000	7 dock north side new tracks
	5,000	10,300	2 & 3 basin railway extensions to enable Yard Services cranes to serve these areas
	3,000	5,000	7 dock north side new tracks
	3,300	9,000	2 & 3 basin railway extensions
1932	2,000	5,000	Roads & railways renewals
1935	2,000	4,000	North & South Yards renewals of roads & railways

From 1891 onwards there appears the commentary that the redemption of the debt to the Great Western (Cornwall) Railway is £10,315. 3s. 11d, which appears to at least 1903.

1938 was the last Navy Estimates before the War. They recommenced in 1946 but without the detail of pre-war.

APPENDIX THREE

TABLE OF FREIGHT SHIPMENTS

	1962	1963	1964	1978	1979	1980	1981*
INCOMING TRUCKS	6177	6117	6457	1459	1147	665	108
Average per Weekday	25	24	26	6	5	3	
Going to:-							
Transhipped to road			1388	540	405	216	
North Yard			2653	349	391	163	
South Yard			1977	457	288	202	
Morice Yard			439	113	63	84	
Loaded with:-							
Timber			788				
Steel			970				
Coal			320				
'Runners' (empties)			182				65
Ships stores			1792				
Other			2405				43
Tonnage incoming			33,600				
Tonnage outgoing			9,400				
Internal truck movements				446	237	182	70

* 1981 figures are for 6 months only

APPENDIX FOUR

LSWR 1919 INSTRUCTIONS

LONDON & SOUTH WESTERN RAILWAY. INSTRUCTION No.7a, 1919
Revised Instructions for working the
KEYHAM DOCKYARD (DEVONPORT) GOVERNMENT RAILWAY.

This is a Government Line, having its junction at the Saltash end of Keyham Station (G.W.R.), and the points in the Main Line are worked from the Keyham Station Signal Box.

The Line is worked on the Train Staff system Between Keyham Junction and the G.W. Office near the Exchange Sidings at Keyham, the staff being a square shaped wooden one, lettered on one side 'Exchange Sidings railway staff', and on the other side 'R.N. Barracks,' and no engine or train must pass between Keyham Junction and the G.W. Office at Exchange Sidings unless the Driver is in possession of the train staff.

Goods trains going to the Dockyard must, when the gates are open and provided the line is clear, back into the Admiralty Siding, which is situated between Keyham Junction and the Royal Naval Barracks, and when the points are reversed the engine must run round the train by way of the loop siding and draw it to the Dockyard, but if the train consists of more than 16 four-wheeled trucks it must be propelled into the Dockyard, and the Guard must travel in the Brake Van, keep a sharp look out and signal to the Driver to proceed steadily.

On arrival at the Exchange Sidings shunting may be proceeded with.

Passenger trains consisting of not more than 5 eight-wheeled and 1 four-wheeled vehicles may be worked to and from the Dockyard by one engine, which will run round the train at the Admiralty Loop. Such trains must not be propelled between the Admiralty Loop and the Dockyard.

Passenger trains consisting of not more than 7 eight-wheeled vehicles may be worked to and from the NAVAL BARRACKS platform by one engine. Such trains may be propelled between Keyham Junction and the Naval Barracks platform in either direction, the engine to run round the empty train at the Keyham Station Loop.

Passenger trains consisting of more than 5 eight-wheeled and 1 four-wheeled vehicles to and from the Dockyard, or exceeding 7 eight-wheeled vehicles to and from the Naval Barracks platform, must be brought to a stand short of the Junction points and the assistant engine detached and placed in the Junction Siding; the train engine will then draw the train over the Junction points, and the assistant engine standing in the Junction Siding must be brought out and attached in the rear. When this has been done the train will be drawn to the Naval Barracks platform, or the Dockyard, as the case may be, with the assistant engine in front, and the train engine at the rear.

On the return journey, when both engines are required to work the train forward, it will be drawn to the main line with the train engine in front and the assistant engine at the rear. The train engine must then be detached and the train drawn clear of the junction points by the assistant engine to permit of the train engine entering the junction siding, after which the train must be set back clear of the Junction points to allow the train engine to come out from the Junction Siding and be attached to the head of the train. When this has been done both engines will haul the train to North Road and the assistant engine work through to Exeter, if necessary, or run light to Friary.

When one engine only is required to work the train from Keyham, this will be done by the engine propelling the train from the Naval Barracks or Dockyard, the other engine being detached and sent 'light' from Keyham to Friary.

All goods trains coming from the Dockyard must be formed in the Dockyard Sidings and brought to a stand before entering the Down Main Line. After permission has been obtained from the Signalman at Keyham, and the points have been set, the train may shunt to the Down Main line, and be drawn to the Up Main line for starting by way of the crossover road which exists between the Keyham Signal Box and the Junction leading from the Dockyard.

The maximum load for a passenger train going to the Dockyard is 15 eight-wheeled vehicles, and for a goods train 35 trucks and a van. The speed of trains in the Dockyard must not exceed five miles an hour.

Traffic for and from the Keyham Dockyard will be worked from and to Devonport, to which station it should be entered.

The keys of the gates leading to the Branch are retained by the Naval Stores Officer (or his representative), His Majesty's Dockyard, Devonport, to whom application must be made by the Devonport Station Master when it is required to take traffic to or from the Dockyard, and he will be held responsible for arranging to clear the traffic as may be required.

The foregoing instructions cancel those appearing on pages 74 and 75 of the Appendix to the Book of Rules and Regulations and the Working Time Tables, dated 1st January, 1911.

WATERLOO STATION,
23rd October, 1919 (V. 32,076.)

GEO. F. WEST,
Superintendant of line.

APPENDIX FIVE

TABLE OF LOCOMOTIVES

NAME	NUMBER	ARRGMT	WH SIZ.	CYL	CYLSIZ.	BLDR	BLDR No	YEAR	ORIG	DISP
		ADMIRALTY (all standard gauge)								
		0-4-TG	4'0"		10x12	AP	143	1865	For WJ	S/S
		0-4-TG	4'0"		10x12	AP	450	1869	N	S/S
		0-4-0ST		OC	7x12	JF	7710	1897	N	S/S
	1	0-4-0ST	3'0½"	OC	12x18	HL	2399	1898	N	SCRAP
	2	0-4-0ST	3'0½"	OC	12x18	HL	2400	1898	N	SCRAP
	3	0-4-0ST		OC	10	Barclays	296	1882	ex SJJ	S/S
	4					HLT	340	1880	assumed	
	5					FE		1884	assumed	
	6	0-4-0CT	2'10"	OC	12x15	HL	2599	1904	N	SCRAP
	7	0-4-0ST	3'0½"	OC	12x18	HL	2820	1910	N	SCRAP
	8	0-4-0ST	3'0½"	OC	12x18	HL	2821	1910	N	SCRAP
	9	0-4-0ST	3'5"	OC	14x22	AB	1406	1915	S/H	SCRAP
	10	0-4-0ST	3'2"	OC	12x20	AB	1379	1914	N	SCRAP
	11	0-4-0ST	3'2"	OC	12x20	AB	1380	1914	N	SCRAP
	12	0-4-0ST	3'3"	OC	14x20	AE	1690	1915	N	SCRAP
	13	0-4-0ST	3'5"	OC	14x22	AB	1397	1915	N	SCRAP
	14	0-4-0ST	3'6"	OC	14x22	HL	3200	1916	N	SCRAP
	15	0-4-0ST	3'6"	OC	14x22	HL	3201	1916	N	SCRAP
	16	0-4-0ST	3'5"	OC	14x22	AB	1516	1919	N	SCRAP
	17	0-4-0ST	3'2"	OC	12x20	AB	2071	1939	N	SCRAP
	18	0-4-0ST	3'2"	OC	12x20	AB	2137	1942	N	SCRAP
	(fmly 19) 2	0-4-0ST	3'2"	OC	12x20	AB	2221	1946	N	PVD
	19	0-4-0ST	3'6½"	OC	14½x22	WB	2962	1950	N	PVD
	4856	4wDM	3'1½"			FH	3737	1955	N	SOLD
	4857	4wDM	3'1½"			FH	3741	1955	N	SCRAP
	4858	4wDM	3'1½"			FH	3744	1955	N	SOLD
	4859	4wDM	3'1½"			FH	3746	1955	N	SOLD
	4860	4wDM	3'1½"			FH	3774	1955	N	SCRAP
	5197	4wDM	3'1½"			FH	3773	1955	N	SCRAP
	5198	4wDM	3'1½"			FH	3747	1955	N	PVD
	5199	4wDM	3'1½"			FH	3775	1955	N	SCRAP
	5200	4wDM	3'1½"			FH	3776	1956	N	PVD
	5332	4wDM	3'1½"			FH	3816	1956	N	SOLD
	9266	4wDM				S&H	7503	1967	N	TF
	10432	0-4-0 DM	3'3"			DC/VF	2184/5265	1945	S/H	
	10433	0-4-0 DM	3'3"			DC/VF	2177/5258	1945	S/H	
		SIR JOHN JACKSON (all standard gauge)								
Glasgow		0-4-0ST	3'0"	OC	10x17	AB	185	1877	TF	SOLD
Burntisland		0-4-0ST	3'2"	OC	12x20	AB	797	1897	TF	TF
Don Jose		0-4-0ST	3'2"	OC	12x20	AB	810	1897	N	S/S
Ethel		0-4-0ST	3'0"	OC	10x18	AB	853	1899	N	S/S
Kathleen		0-4-0ST	3'0"	OC	10x18	AB	867	1900	N	S/S
Victoria		0-4-0ST	3'2"	OC	12x20	AB	887	1901	N	SOLD
Dover		0-4-0ST	3'0"	OC	10x18	AB	891	1901	N	SOLD
Hamoaze		0-4-0ST	3'0"	OC	10x18	Barclays	229	1876	S/H	SOLD
Middlesbrough		0-4-0ST		OC	10	Barclays	296	1882	S/H	to Adm No3
Maggie		0-4-0ST	2'9"	OC	10x16	HC	287	1887	S/H	SOLD
Flixton		0-4-0ST	2'6"	OC	9x15	HC	293	1887	S/H	S/S
Keyham		0-6-0ST	3'6½"	IC	15X20	HC	318	1889	S/H	SOLD
Swansea		0-6-0ST	3'4"	IC	14x18	HE	1	1865	S/H	SOLD
Tamar		0-4-0ST		OC	9x14	HE	360	1884	S/H	TF
Devonport		0-6-0T		IC	15x20	HE	401	1886	S/H	TF

APPENDIX FIVE
continued

TABLE OF LOCOMOTIVES

NAME	NUMBER	ARRGMT	WH SIZ.	CYL	CYLSIZ.	BLDR	BLDR No	YEAR	ORIG	DISP
\multicolumn{11}{c}{**SIR JOHN JACKSON (continued)**}
Manchester		0-6-0ST		IC	14x18	HE	437	1887	S/H	TF
Dorothy		0-4-0ST	3'0½"	OC	12x18	HL	2329	1896	N	S/S
Clyde		0-4-0ST	2'9"	OC	9x14	MW	714	1879	S/H	TF
Accrington		0-6-0ST	3'4"	IC	14x20	MW	951	1885	S/H	SOLD
Lord Roberts		0-4-0ST	2'9"	OC	10x16	MW	1018	1887	S/H	S/S
Torcross		0-4-0ST	2'9"	OC	10x16	MW	1036	1887	S/H	SOLD
Tyne		0-4-0ST	2'9"	OC	10x16	MW	1051	1888	S/H	S/S
Lord Nelson		0-4-0ST	3'0"	OC	12x18	MW	1090	1888	S/H	S/S
Mount Edgecumbe		0-4-0ST	2'9"	OC	10x16	MW	1342	1897	S/H	S/S
Westminster		0-6-0T	3'0"	IC	13x20	SS	3474	1888	S/H	TF
\multicolumn{11}{c}{**GRANT LYON EAGRE Ltd (standard gauge)**}
		4wDM				S&H	7510	1967	TF	TF
\multicolumn{11}{c}{**B SUNLEY & CO (all 2'0" gauge)**}
		4wBE				WR	1395	1939	N	S/S
		4wBE				WR	1396	1939	N	S/S
		4wBE				WR	1397	1939	N	S/S
		4wDM(?)				R&R	85	1939	N	S/S
		4wDM(?)				R&R	89	1939	N	S/S
		4wDM(?)				R&R	90	1939	N	S/S
\multicolumn{11}{c}{**EDMUND NUTTALL, Sons & Co (London) Ltd. (standard gauge)**}
		4wDM				RH	186314	1937	N	TF
		4wDM				RH	186316	1937	N	TF

Key

0-4(6)-0	four (six) driving wheels linked by external coupling rods
4w	four driving wheels driven internally
BE	Battery electric
DM	Diesel mechanical
DH	Diesel hydraulic
OC	Outside cylinders
IC	Inside cylinders
ST	Side tank
T	Tank
CT	Crane tank
S/H	Secondhand
N	New
S/S	Sold or scrapped, disposal unknown
TF	Transferred
SOLD	Sold from site
PVD	Preserved
AB	Andrew Barclay, Sons & Co. Ltd., Caledonia Works, Kilmarnock
AE	Avonside Engineering Co. Ltd., Bristol
Barclays	Barclays & Co., Riverside Works, Kilmarnock
DC/VF	Drewry Car Co. Ltd., London/Vulcan Foundry Ltd., Newton-le-Willows
FE	Falcon Engine & Car Works Ltd., Loughborough
FH	F. C. Hibberd & Co. Ltd., Park Royal
HC	Hudswell Clark & Co. Ltd., Leeds
HE	Hunslet Engine Co. Ltd., Leeds
HL	Hawthorn Leslie & Co. Ltd., Newcastle upon Tyne
HLT	Hughes Locomotive & Tramway Engine Works Ltd., Loughborough
JF	John Fowler & Co Ltd, Leeds
MW	Manning Wardle & Co Ltd., Leeds
RH	Ruston & Hornsby Ltd., Lincoln
R&R	Ransomes & Rapier Ltd., Ipswich
SS	Sharp, Stewart & Co. Ltd., Glasgow
S&H	Strachan & Henshaw Ltd., Bristol
WB	W. G. Bagnall Ltd., Stafford
WR	Wingrove & Rogers Ltd., Liverpool

APPENDIX SIX

TABLE OF ROLLING STOCK

No.	WHEELS	BODY
PASSENGER		
1	4	workmen's single compt.
9	4	3 compt
10	4	workmen's single compt.
13	4	workmean's single compt.
16	4	3 compt
26	4	workmen's single compt. (?)
55	4	workmen's single compt.
137	4	workmen's single compt.
180	4	workmen's single compt.
341	4	3 compt
342	4	3 compt
344	4	workmen's single compt.

No.	WHEELS	BODY	LOAD	NOTES
GOODS				
4	4	40 T flat	40-0-0	Beyond economical repair 12/79
8	4	tank		
13	4	closed van	6-0-0	for disp 11/82
14	4	closed van	6-0-0	for disp 11/82
15	4	closed van	6-0-0	for disp 11/82
16	4	closed van	6-0-0	for disp 11/82
17	4	closed van	6-0-0	for disp 11/82
19	?	high box (7 plank)		
22	4	7 plank open		for disp 11/82
26	?	van		
27	4	flat		
51	?	plate		for disp 2/84
52	?	plate		for disp 2/84
53	?	plate		for disp 2/84
56	?	plate		for disp 2/84
58	4	closed van		
73	4	flat		in pass. consist 1964
75	?	van		for disp 11/82
76	?	van		for disp 11/82
77	?	van		for disp 11/82
95	?	flat		
104	4	flat		
112	4	flat		
121	?	flat wood		
135	4	7 plank		
140	?	flat		
147	4	3 plank		
151	4	7 plank open	4-5-0	Axle boxes dated 1912. Appears in 'Force 10' film
178	4	closed van		
180	?	van		
192	?	high box (7 plank)		
229	?	high box (7 plank)		
240	?	van		
241	4	5 plank open		
248	4	6 plank open		
255	4	4 plank open		
265	?	flat wood		
291	4	7 plank open		
334	4+4	bogie well	40-0-0	25T in well
335	4+4	crocodile		for disp 3/84
336	4+4	tube 4 plank open		Appears in 'Force 10' film. For disp 11/82
337	?	BBC (?)		for disp 3/84
342	?	van		
344	?	van		
347	4	flat	40-0-0	
353	?	flat iron		
356	4+4	crocodile flat		
361	4+4+4	girder set		3 flats + beam
387	4	6 plank open		
392	4+4	gondola flat bogie		
393	4+4+4+4	gun truck		
419	4	closed van		'not for tunnel working'
437	4	flat		in pass. consist
450	?	high box (7 plank)		
451	4	7 plank open	6-5-0	Appears in 'Force 10' film.
452	?	high box (7 plank)		
457	?	half box (4 plank)		
458	4	4 plank		
459	4	4 plank	5-6-0	
642	4	4 plank		
615	4	4 plank		
646	4	4 plank		for disp 11/82
667	4	7 plank open		
683	?	half box (4 plank)		
686	4	4 plank open		
688	?	flat wood		
692	?	flat wood		
695	?	flat wood		
696	?	flat wood		
699	?	flat wood		
49004	4	guards van		vacuum fitted
95105	?	warflat		for disp 4/84
95126	?	warflat		for disp 4/84

also up to 18 other items purchased by Plym Valley Railway which have not been identified and have disappeared pre 1992.

APPENDIX SEVEN

TABLE OF SHUNTING CRANES

YARD No.	YEAR	MANUFACTURER	WKS No.	YARD	ENGINE	SIZE	REMARKS
		ADMIRALTY	**RAIL**	**GAUGE**	**CRANES**		
	1890	Grafton	178		steam	5T	
	1892	Grafton	253		steam	7T	
	1892	Grafton	391		steam	5T	disp to Llanelly Construction 1936
	1897	Grafton	479		steam	5T	
	1900	Grafton	631		steam	5T	
	1903	Grafton	849		steam	7T	
	1903	Grafton	854		steam	10T	
	1903	Grafton	855		steam	10T	
	1906	HJ Coles	421		steam	7T	
	1906	HJ Coles	422		steam	7T	
	1909	Grafton	1178		steam	10T	
	1909	Grafton	1179		steam	10T	
	1909	Grafton	1180		steam	10T	
	1909	Grafton	1181		steam	10T	
	1910	Jos. Booth	2345A		steam	3T	
	1910	Jos. Booth	2345B		steam	3T	
	1914	Jos. Booth	2813A		steam	10T	
	1914	Jos. Booth	2813B		steam	10T	
	1915	Grafton	1614		steam	7T	
	1915	Grafton	1615		steam	7T	
	1915	Grafton	1646		steam	7T	disp to Plymouth & Devonport Shipbreaking
	1915	Grafton	1647		steam	7T	disp to Borough of Plymouth
	1915	Grafton	1648		steam	7T	
	1915	Grafton	1649		steam	7T	
	1916	Stothert & Pitt	B4107		steam	1½T	
	1916	T Smith	8822		steam	1½T	
	1916	T Smith	8823		steam	1½T	
	1918	Grafton	1808		steam	10T	
	1918	Grafton	1809		steam	10T	
	1931	T Smith	11640		steam	5T	
	1939	T Smith	12968		steam	3T	
173	1940	Taylor & Hubbard	1431		steam	5T	
174	1940	Grafton	2561		steam	10T	scrapped 8/73
175	1940	Grafton	2555		steam		
176	1940	Grafton	2554	S	steam	6T	scrapped 28.2.76
186	1940	T Smith	13639		steam		
258	1943	Taylor & Hubbard	1520		steam	5T	
259	1943	Taylor & Hubbard	1521		steam	5T	
270	1942	Grafton	2597		steam	7T	
331	1942	Grafton	2677		steam	10T	broken for spares 1967
332	1942	Grafton	2678		steam	10T	
353	1946	Grafton	2810	N	steam	3T	
354		Coles			steam		
370	1947	Grafton	2822		steam	10T	
388	1947	Grafton	2826	S	steam	6T	
410	1949	Grafton	2842	N	steam	6T	
411	1950	Grafton	2841		steam	10T	
412				N	steam		
428	1949	Grafton	2854	N	steam	6T	
429	1950	Grafton	2853		steam	10T	
	1950	Grafton	2883		steam		
444	1952	Grafton	2887		steam		
447	1952	T Smith	19393		diesel		
448	1952	T Smith	19394		diesel		
4896	1954	T Smith	23507	S	Foden diesel	3T	broken for spares Dec 1967
4897	1954	T Smith	23508	S	Foden diesel	3T	
4898	1954	T Smith	23509	N	Foden diesel	3T	
4899	1954	T Smith	23510	N	Foden diesel	3T	
4900	1954	T Smith	23511	N	Foden diesel	3T	in use 10/81. 5 basin NE
4901	1954	T Smith	23512	N	Foden diesel	3T	
4902	1956	T Smith	23513	S>N	Foden diesel	6T	spare 10/81
4903	1956	T Smith	23514	S	Foden diesel	6T	in use 10/81. Sawmills
4904	1956	T Smith	23515	S	Foden diesel	6T	in use 10/81. Chain Cable Pound

APPENDIX SEVEN
continued

TABLE OF SHUNTING CRANES

YARD No.	YEAR	MANUFACTURER	WKS No.	YARD	ENGINE	SIZE	REMARKS
\multicolumn{8}{c}{**ADMIRALTY RAIL GAUGE CRANES**}
4905	1956	T Smith	23516	N	Foden diesel	6T	to S 1.10.74
4906	1956	T Smith	23517	N	Foden diesel	6T	to S 1.10.74. in use 10/81: 3 slip
4909	1956	T Smith		S	Foden diesel	6T	
5184	1956	T Smith	23806	N	Foden diesel	3T	
5185	1956	T Smith	23807	S	Foden diesel	3T	
5186	1956	T Smith	23808	N	Foden diesel	3T	
5187	1956	T Smith	23809	S	Foden diesel	3T	
5188	1956	T Smith	23810	S	Foden diesel	3T	conv. to 6T 11/67
5189	1956	T Smith	23811	S	Foden diesel	3T	
5190	1956	T Smith	23812	S	Foden diesel	6T	in use 10/81. South Yard Shot Blast Plant
5191	1956	T Smith	23813	S	Foden diesel	6T	spare 10/81
5192	1956	T Smith	23814	S	Foden diesel	6T	in use 10/81. Bouy Wharf. Replaced by 9282
5193	1956	T Smith	23815	N	Foden diesel	6T	in use 10/81: 5 basin SW. to PVR 1985
5194	1956	T Smith	23816	N	Foden diesel	6T	
7695				N	Foden diesel	3T	
7696				N	Foden diesel	3T	in use 10/81. 9 dock E
9103	1967	T Smith	26459	N	Perkins diesel	10T	in use 10/81: 4 basin E. removed 1990
9282	1968	T Smith		S	Perkins diesel	10T	spare 10/81. Replaced by 5192

In addition an Asset Register reference book lists the following Yard No's as rail gauge steam cranes but further identification has not been possible:
2, 9, 10, 20, 21, 24-53, 57-65, 76, 77, 150, 153-155, 330, 413, 475-479.

SIR JOHN JACKSON

STANDARD GAUGE

YEAR	MANUFACTURER	WKS No.	ENGINE	SIZE
1895	T Smith	4982	steam	5T
1895	T Smith	4983	steam	5T
1895	T Smith	4984	steam	5T
1896	T Smith	5074	steam	5T
1896	T Smith	5122	steam	5T
1896	T Smith	5171	steam	5T
1896	T Smith	5172	steam	5T
1896	J Booth	978A	steam	5T
1896	J Booth	978B	steam	5T
1896	J Booth	978C	steam	5T
1896	J Booth	978D	steam	5T
1896	J Booth	978E	steam	5T
1897	T Smith	5225	steam	5T
1897	T Smith	5226	steam	5T
1898	T Smith	5500	steam	5T
1898	T Smith	5501	steam	5T
1898	T Smith	5502	steam	5T
1898	T Smith	5503	steam	5T
1898	T Smith	5504	steam	5T
1898	T Smith	5505	steam	5T

STANDARD & 7ft GAUGE ON SAME AXLE (used as steam Navvy's)

YEAR	MANUFACTURER	WKS No.	ENGINE	SIZE
1896	J Booth	997	steam	5T
1896	J Booth	998	steam	5T
1896	J Booth	1047A	steam	7T
1896	J Booth	1047B	steam	7T
1897	J Booth	1074A	steam	5T
1897	J Booth	1074B	steam	5T
1897	J Booth	1074C	steam	5T
1897	J Booth	1074D	steam	5T

SOURCES & ACKNOWLEDGEMENTS

One lasting legacy of the Luftwaffe's attentions to Plymouth in the Second World War was the loss of much of the city's documents, both civil and military. Fortunately, older documents had already been deposited in the national archive, and it is these that form the main source of early information for this book. Although access to the items at the Public Record Office at Kew can be a tedious experience, the gems that are to be eventualy found make it all worthwhile. I am particularly grateful to D.W. Winkworth for guiding me into it's system. The helpful staff of other Record Offices, viz: Devon and West Devon, House of Lords and the Royal Archives is acknowledged. But as referred to above, the paucity of information, and particularly photographs, prior to the Second World War is regretted.

My connection with Devonport Dockyard dates from 1988, hence much of what has been written here pre-dates me. I am therefore grateful to colleagues and former employees who were kind enough to make time to relate their observations of what to them was common-place, but unknown to me. It is a shame to single out the few, but to all I am grateful. In particular Andy Endacott, Mike Daly, Dave Down, the late Stan Greenwood, Chris Horsham, Dave Kiver, Brian Mennie, Mike Parsons, Fred Paul, Dave Rogers, Harold Ross, Chris Trethewey, Bernard Taylor.

The assistance of Devonport Management Ltd., since 1987 the managing contractor of Devonport Dockyard, and now to become the owner, is gratefully acknowledged.

Many official records are now coming into the public domain, and the Plymouth Naval Base Museum (formerly known as the Devonport Dockyard Museum) has become a repository for much relating to the Yard. My first sight of their archive was a huge pile of dockets, albums, papers, and drawings, heaped in a back room. l am pleased that a formal basis for preserving this valuable archive is now in place, and a curator appointed. Other organisations hold records which were consulted and thanks to their officers viz: Branch Line Society (N.J. Hill); the World War Two Railway Study Group; the LNER Wagon Group; Great Western Museum (Tim Bryan); Institution of Civil Engineers; Ministry of Defence Whitehall Library; Principal Supply & Transport Officer (Navy) (Gordon Mott and Roger Beaumont); RNEC Manadon (Jim Quibell); National Railway Museum (Phil Atkins); Mitchell Library, Glasgow; Royal Commission for Historic Monuments of England (Liz Churchman); TSW-FTA (Graham Spink); Devon Library Services at the Naval & Local History Reference Library, and the Railway Studies Collection (former librarian Don Steggles), and also my local branch library at Crownhill who cheerfully ordered the most obscure books for me.

The help and guidance of the Officers and my fellow Members of the Industial Locomotive Society and the Industrial Railway Society, steered me to find all sorts of information in their own and others possession.

Then many individuals who patiently helped me in all manner of ways: John Binding; Harold D Bowtell; Mike Christensen; Larry Crosier; R.A. Cooke; Michael Cook; Dame Janet Fookes MP; Dave Foracre; John Gardner; Roger Hateley; Richard Hawkins; Brian Henderson; Ian Hutchinson; Graham Johnson; R.C. Riley; Don Townsley; Geoff Horsman; Russell Wear; Peter Briddon; my friends in the Plymouth Railway Circle; and others.

Finally two special acknowledgements. Firstly to Terry Waldron who unselfishly gave time to help, particularly with the visits to Kew and thus provided two man-days of effort at each visit. Lastly to my wife Diane, who allowed domestic matters to be ignored for so long while this was produced. To her this book is dedicated.

FURTHER READING

For a fuller history of Devonport Dockyard, the reader is directed to :

The Devonport Dockyard Story by the late Lt. Cdr. K.V. Burns; Maritime Books.
The Royal Dockyards 1690-1850 by Jonathan G. Coad; Scolar Press.
The History of HMS Drake by Peter Brimacombe; for HMS Drake by Mor Marketing.

Railways in the area are extensively documented. General titles are:

A Regional History of the Railways of Great Britain; Vol. 1; The West Country by David St John Thomas; David & Charles.
The Railways of Devon by Martin Smith; Ian Allan.
An Illustrated History of Plymouth's Railways by Martin Smith; Irwell Press.

INDEX

Accidents **57, 60, 61, 64, 73, 77, 85, 127**
Admiralty, or Drake, or Barracks, Platform **36, 37, 39, 65, 74, 87, 91**
Auction **55**
Barracks: Keyham, or Seamen's **36, 37, 71**
Barracks Platform *see Admiralty Platform*
Bodmin & Wenford Railway **101, 102**
Broad Gauge **19, 21, 25, 37, 56, 61**
Cornwall Railway **21 et seq., 79**
Cranes **139**
Devonport, or South, Yard **19, 24, 29, 30, 57**
Devonport Management Limited **66-68, 86**
Drake Platform *see Admiralty Platform*
William Drew (Contractor) **22**
Exchange Sidings **40, 55, 56, 69, 76, 77, 92, 113**
Freight **75 et seq, 87 et seq**
Great Western Railway **36, 61, 79, 80**
GunWharf, or MoriceYard **6, 7, 12-14, 17-19, 26, 60**
Sir John Jackson (Contractor) **46 et seq., 103-104, 110, 121, 125-128, 141**
W Jackson (Contractor) **16, 97**
Keyham **24, 41, 42**
Keyham, or North, Yard **7, 9, 10, 13, 22, 36, 59**
Keyham Junction **40, 41, 43, 44, ,79, 92, 94**
Keyham Station **43, 44, 79, 82**
Livery **97, 108, 131**
Locomotive Sheds **33, 61, 62, 97**
Locomotives **17, 19, 50, 51, 55, 57, 59, 61, 62, 67, 89, 90, 97 et seq.**
London & South Western Railway **24, 26, 88**
Millbay Station (GWR) **24**
Morice Yard *see Gun Wharf*
Narrow Gauge **17, 54, 57, 61**
Narrows **34**
North Corner (Cornwall Beach) **6, 7**
North Yard *see Keyham Yard*
Passenger train **36, 63, 71 et seq., 132**
Permanent Way **23, 54, 63, 93 et seq.**
J. Pethick (Contractor) **19, 20**
Platforms **59**
Plym Valley Railway **136, 141**
Quadrangle **8, 16, 25, 94**
Rolling Stock **73, 131 et seq.**
Royalty **55, 74, 122**
Signal Boxes **40, 84, 105**
Signalling **32, 58, 79 et seq., 83 et seq.**
Standard Gauge **24, 26, 29, 37**
South Devon Railway **21**
South Yard *see Devonport Yard*
Southern Railway **79, 80, 88**
Turntables **24. 35. 54, 94 et seq.**
Tunnel **9 et seq., 25, 27-29, 31, 32, 65, 77, 83**
Weston Mill Viaduct **22, 26, 40**